MW01234840

MASTER YOUR EMOTIONS FOR BEGINNERS

THE COMPLETE GUIDE TO DEVELOP EMOTIONAL INTELLIGENCE

Table of contents

INTRODUCTION

As we travel through our day by day lives, we experience an assortment of emotions (which we frequently call "sentiments"). Emotions are abstract conditions of being that, physiologically, include physiological excitement, psychological examination and intellectual procedures, emotional encounters, and expressive conduct. Emotions are frequently the main thrust behind inspiration (regardless of whether positive or negative) and are communicated and imparted through a wide scope of practices, for example, manner of speaking and non-verbal communication.

Our psychological evaluation of a circumstance is educated by our encounters, foundation, and culture. In this way, various people may have diverse emotional encounters of comparable circumstances. Be that as it may, the capacity to create and perceive outward emotional appearances is by all accounts general. All things considered, societies contrast in how frequently and under what conditions it is "alright" to communicate different emotions, just as how different articulations of emotions are deciphered.

Emotions accept an obvious activity in human life. They can play out various limits. They can give energizing bases to all of our exercises. They can he normally adaptable and go about as protective framework as when a frightened individual escapes from a wellspring of hazard. They can be moreover a wellspring of bliss and wretchedness. Life's happiness is on an exceptionally essential level buildup with the fulfillment of our emotions. So to speak, it will, in general, be said that the fulfillment of human life itself is built up in emotions. Suitable sublimation, confinement, and control of emotions can be not simply the best bit of a person's preparation yet furthermore his refinement and culture. Emotions can be rising or ruining. The find a good pace of life starts from eager experiences. Emotion is an unusual technique for acting. An eager response is the unitary consequence of different complex physiological limits in our body structure, for instance, working of endocrine organs and other natural techniques inside the body. An enthusiastic response is an

integrated reaction of the whole character. An inclination may be energized by an event in the outside world or inside the individual himself, "The reason for experience is excited, '" and thusly feeling lies at the establishment of existence. A broad bit of man's character is known through his convictions, attitudes, sentiments, and structures, and it is emotions that go into the production of all these. Everyone will experience emotions in various habits, anyway moderately, not many of us understand how to oversee them or how to oversee them. Emotion controls both thought and lead. Outfit people with one of the most impressive drives towards creative development. "Since emotions are a provision of nature, it would be tactlessness to ignore them or to2destroy them". The components of individual relations in the family and outside are altogether coordinated by emotions. If the human mind continues in a stirred up energetic state for a long time, various dismal conditions, both mental and physiological, may follow. Correspondingly if commanding emotions are smothered for long it's repercussions for direct may be totally serious, "Eager adjustment is a fused case of activity".^ "The specific reactions of modification depending on the possibility of the emotive condition, its individual's view, such character factors as age, sex, getting, shortcoming and motivation and the possibility of the experiences and changes energized clearly by the impression of the emotive situation," ^If an individual is genuinely solid, he can

Conform to the "Changing solicitations and will be most consistent with singular happiness, effectiveness, and social welfare." If he is maladjusted, by then he will be a danger to the overall population; A sound energetic advancement is central for an individual to be really merry and socially useful. The reason for preparing itself is enthusiastic, and the education of emotions in kids is a noteworthy endeavor for the two watchmen and instructors.

The Stages of Emotional Development

During the prior long periods of life, our ability for emotional encounters, as we develop more established, offers an approach to reason, yet additionally, the technique for communicating feeling experiences changes and turns out to be progressively controlled by social and social standards of conduct. In other words, our emotional expressions become increasingly conventionalized. Social and cultural pressures teach to keep his inclination to himself. In the course of the emotional improvement of children, there are sure stages that sire transitional and include strains and emergencies.

As it has been psychologically

Decided even ordinary youngsters discover trouble in making a smooth change starting with one phase then onto the next. So while it is imperative to consider the emotional improvement from birth to development,' it is especially essential to read these basic focuses for a legitimate comprehension of the components in question.

In a developing youngster's interest is on the expansion, and it drives him to peculiar and new experiences, For a developing kid, the hover of emotional encounters extend and it keeps remembering for it increasingly more of articles and circumstances towards which he may become emotionally related. At that point, emotional life turns out to be progressively organized and mind-boggling as the youngster develops and learns.

"Emotional advancement relies upon the youngster's expanding capacity to choose and respond to a more extensive assortment and more noteworthy multifaceted nature of boosts and to organize, coordinate, and intelligently adjust his reactions." The kid's emotional reactions are getting instructed nearly from its hour birth. Healthy emotional perspectives ought to be created at various phases of a person's improvement.

WHAT EMOTIONS ARE

Emotions are organic states related to the sensory system expedited by neurophysiological changes differently connected with considerations, sentiments, social reactions, and a level of delight or dismay.

Emotions likewise imply including physiological parts, social or emotional names (anger, shock, and so on.), expressive body activities, and the evaluation of circumstances and settings.

Emotions can be events (e.g., frenzy) or manners (e.g., antagonistic vibe), and fleeting (e.g., anger) or extensive (e.g., melancholy). All emotions as existing on a continuum of power. Along these lines, fear may go from mellow worry to dread, or disgrace may go from straightforward humiliation to harmful disgrace. Emotions have been depicted as comprising of a planned arrangement of reactions, which may incorporate verbal, physiological, conduct, and neural systems.

Emotions have been ordered, with certain connections existing among emotions and some immediate contrary energies existing. Emotions are practical or useless and contend every single useful feeling has benefits.

Emotions are extreme sentiments that are aimed at a person or thing. Then again, the feeling can be utilized to allude to states that are mellow (as in irritated or content) and to states that are not aimed at anything (as in uneasiness and discouragement). Emotions imply the consequence of a subjective and cognizant procedure, which happens in light of a body framework reaction to a trigger.

For a great many people, sentiments and emotions are especially the equivalents. Normally, we would see them as equivalent words; two words with a similar significance. Be that as it may, despite the fact that they are reliant on one another, emotions and sentiments are somewhat various things.

Emotions portray physiological states and are produced intuitively. Typically, they are self-sufficient real reactions to the certain outside or inside occasions. On the other hand, sentiments are abstract encounters of emotions and are driven by cognizant considerations and reflections. This implies we can have emotions without having sentiments. Nonetheless, we essentially can't have emotions without having emotions.

It's essential to recognize what a feeling is and what an inclination is. While the two are interconnected, there's a greater contrast than you may understand. It's unquestionably something that shocked me when I started with my examination.

Emotions – Emotions are viewed as 'lower level' reactions. They initially happen in the subcortical territories of the cerebrum, for example, the amygdala and the ventromedial prefrontal cortices. These territories are answerable for delivering biochemical responses that directly affect your physical state.

Emotions are coded into our DNA and are thought to have created as an approach to assist us with reacting rapidly to various ecological dangers, much like our 'battle or flight' reaction. The amygdala has additionally been appeared to assume a job in the arrival of synapses that are fundamental for memory, which is the reason emotional recollections are frequently more grounded and simpler to review.

Emotions have a more grounded physical establishing than sentiments meaning analysts discover them simpler to gauge equitably through physical signals, for example, blood flow, pulse, mind action, outward appearances, and non-verbal communication.

Sentiments – Emotions are viewed as going before sentiments, which will, in general, be our responses to the various emotions we experience.
Where emotions can have an increasingly summed up understanding over all people, sentiments are progressively abstract and are affected by our own encounters and translations of our reality dependent on those encounters.

Sentiments happen in the neocortical districts of the mind and are the following stage by the way we react to our emotions as a person. Since they are so abstract, they can't be estimated the manner in which emotions can.

KINDS OF EMOTIONS

27 discrete emotions named as in the following rundown:

- Admiration

- Adoration

- Aesthetic Appreciation

- Amusement

- Anxiety

- Awe

- Awkwardness

- Boredom

- Calmness

- Confusion

- Craving

- Disgust

- Empathetic torment

- Entrancement

- Envy

- Excitement

- Fear

- Horror

- Interest

- Joy

- Nostalgia

- Romance

- Sadness

- Satisfaction

- Sexual want

- Sympathy

- Triumph

Emotions are a basic piece of what your identity is, yet they can be chaotic, entangled, and out and out confounding now and then. Realizing how to name them and discussion about them — with both yourself as well as other people — is a key piece of creating emotional health.

Luckily, you don't need to explore the way toward recognizing your emotions alone.

EMOTIONS ARE BREAK DOWN INTO 6 MAIN CATEGORIES:

1. Enjoyment

2. Sadness

3. Fear

4. Anger

5. Disgust

6. surprises

Remember, this is only one method for classifying emotions. Here's a glance at what every one of these six classes includes.

1. Enjoyment

People commonly prefer to feel cheerful, quiet, and great. You may communicate these sentiments by grinning, giggling, or entertaining yourself.

You may feel enjoyment when:

- you feel close and associated with people you care about

- you have a sense of security and secure

- you're accomplishing something that triggers tactile delight

- you're invested in an action

- you feel loose and settled

The most effective method to discuss it

A few words you can use to portray various types of enjoyment include:

- happiness

- love

- relief

- contentment

- amusement

- joy

- pride

- excitement

- peace

- satisfaction

- compassion

On the off chance that enjoyment and its related sentiments feel tricky, attempt to investigate different emotions or emotions are disrupting everything, for example,

- trouble concentrating on what's going on in the present

- worry

- stress

- a low or on edge temperament

2. Pity

Everybody feels pitiful now and again. This feeling may identify with a particular occasion, for example, a misfortune or dismissal. However, in different cases, you may have no clue why you feel miserable.

The most effective method to discuss it

At the point when you're pitiful, you may depict yourself as feeling:

- lonely

- heartbroken

- gloomy

- disappointed

- hopeless

- grieved

- unhappy

- lost

- troubled

- resigned

- miserable

Misery can be difficult to shake, however, relying upon your circumstance. These tips may help:

• Mourn. Grieving is a typical piece of sorrow. Regardless of whether you're attempting to recuperate from a misfortune, separation, change, or inability to accomplish an objective, recognizing your misfortune can assist you with tolerating and work through it. Everybody laments in their own particular manner, so make the right decision to you. It may assist with discussing the agony you're in, yet it likewise may help just to express them imaginatively.

• Do something significant. Planning something to help other people or offer back to society can assist you with feeling increasingly associated with others. In the event that you've as of late, lost somebody you thought about, consider completing a venture they thought about or giving your opportunity to a reason they bolstered.

• Reach out for help. This is actually quite difficult when you're on a low point. Attempt to recollect the people in your life who care for you and likely need to support you. The agony of grief eases in time, regardless of whether you can't envision that right now.

On the off chance that your misery waits or starts to affect day by day life significantly and makes it difficult to work, go to class, or keep up your connections, it might assist with conversing with an advisor.

3. Fear

Fear happens when you sense any sort of danger. Contingent upon that apparent risk, fear can run from mellow to serious.

Remember that the degree of fear you feel doesn't generally coordinate with the power of the risk. For instance, in the event that you live with uneasiness, you may feel fear around circumstances that don't really present quite a bit of danger — however that doesn't make the fear any less genuine.

Step by step instructions to discuss it

Fear can cause you to feel:

- worried

- doubtful

- nervous

- anxious

- terrified

- panicked

- horrified

- desperate

- confused

- stressed

Fear is an absolutely ordinary feeling — and one that probable shielded your precursors from being eaten alive — however, there are things you can do to battle it:

• Confront fear as opposed to avoiding it. In case you're apprehensive about something, regardless of whether it's a genuine conversation, meeting new people, or driving, it's normal to need to avoid the wellspring of your fear. Be that as it may, this can regularly simply aggravate your fear. Rather, attempt to confront your fear securely. For instance, in the event that you out of nowhere build up a fear of driving, get back in your vehicle, and drive again immediately. Stick near and dear from the outset in the event that it helps, yet don't avoid it.

• Distract yourself from your fear. Now and then, fear can turn out to be overpowering to such an extent that it's difficult to consider whatever else. Yet, ruminating, or letting similar considerations happen, again and again, can negatively affect your emotional state. It can likewise aggravate fear. In the event that you feel yourself focusing on stress or wellspring of stress, have a go at something diverting. Tune in to a book recording or digital broadcast, cook with another formula you need to focus on, or take a walk or run with some empowering music.

• Consider the fear of legitimately. Pause for a minute to consider your fear. Is there anything you can do about it? Can it really hurt you? What's the most noticeably awful thing that could occur if your fear worked out? What might you do in that situation? Knowing how you would manage your fear can assist you with feeling less apprehensive.

Try not to get debilitated if these tips appear to be unimaginable or overpowering — they can be difficult to achieve alone. Think about working with a specialist, who can assist you with exploring alarm assaults, fears, nervousness, and other psychological wellness issues around fear.

4. Anger

Anger, for the most part, happens when you experience some kind of foul play. This experience can cause you to feel undermined, caught, and unfit to safeguard yourself. Numerous people consider it angers a pessimistic thing, yet it's a typical feeling that can enable you to know when a circumstance has gotten lethal.

The most effective method to discuss it

Words you may utilize when you feel furious include:

- annoyed

- frustrated

- peeved

- contrary

- bitter

- infuriated

- irritated

- mad

- cheated

- vengeful

- insulted

There is a lot of approaches to manage anger, a large number of which can mess up you and people around you.

Whenever you wind up while throwing a mini tantrum, attempt these tips for overseeing anger in a progressively gainful manner:

• Take a break. At the point when you feel disappointed, putting some separation among yourself and the circumstance upsetting, you can assist you with avoiding in-the-minute responses or furious upheavals. Have a go at going for a stroll or tuning in to a quieting melody. While away, take a couple of moments to consider what's causing your anger. Does the circumstance have another point of view? Would you be able to improve?

• Express your anger productively. You may avoid discussing your anger to help forestall struggle. Disguising can appear to be a sheltered methodology, yet your anger can putrefy, and you may wind up nursing resentment. This can influence your relational connections just as your emotional prosperity. Rather, set aside an effort to chill in the event that you need it. At that point, take a stab at communicating your emotions serenely and deferentially.

• Focus on finding an answer. Anger is frequently hard to manage in light of the fact that it causes you to feel vulnerable. Attempting to take care of the problem that is causing your anger can help calm this dissatisfaction. You will most likely be unable to fix each circumstance that drives you mad. However, you can use as a rule plan something for achieving some improvement. Ask others included what they think and work together. You can likewise have a go at approaching your friends and family for their information. Alternate points of view can assist you with considering arrangements you might not have seen yourself.

Everybody blows up occasionally. Be that as it may, on the off chance that you have a feeling that you have anger issues, a specialist can assist you with creating effective instruments for managing these emotions.

5. Disgust

You normally experience disgust as a response to horrendous or undesirable circumstances. Like anger, sentiments of disgust can assist with shielding from things you need to avoid.

It can likewise present problems in the event that it drives you to hate certain people, including yourself, or circumstances that aren't really awful for you.

Step by step instructions to discuss it

Disgust may make you feel:

- dislike

- revulsion

- loathing

- disapproving

- offended

- horrified

- uncomfortable

- nauseated

- disturbed

- withdrawal

- aversion

Disgust can occur as a characteristic reaction to something you despise. In certain circumstances, you should work through or beat your disgust. These methodologies can help:

• Practice sympathy. It's entirely expected to feel awkward when confronting things you fear or don't comprehend. Numerous people loathe being around wiped out people, for instance. On the off chance that you feel upset when pondering wiped out people, take a stab at investing some energy with an unwell companion or adored one or offering to enable them to out. It's critical to find a way to ensure your own health, so ensure they aren't infectious first.

• Focus on the conduct, not the individual. In the event that somebody you care for accomplishes something that annoys or disgusts you, you may object and respond by pulling back, pushing them away, or blowing up. Be that as it may, rather, you may take a stab at conversing with that individual. For instance, if your sister smokes, avoid hacking boisterously or offering pointed remarks about the smell of stale tobacco. Rather, disclose to her that tobacco smoke causes you to feel debilitated and that you're worried about her health. Offer to assist her with stopping or work with her on discovering support.

• Expose yourself slowly. A few things may simply make you feel sick, regardless. Possibly you can't stand any sort of frightening little animal yet wish you could have a go at planting. To battle disgust over what worms look like, you may begin by finding out about them and taking a gander at pictures of them. In the event that you stress over them jumping on your hands, you could take a stab at wearing planting gloves. In the event that you don't care for watching them move, you could take a stab at observing short video cuts about worms to become acclimated to them before observing them, in actuality.

On the off chance that you feel solid abhorrence toward a gathering of people, a particular individual, or toward yourself, think about conversing with a specialist regarding your emotions (seeing a topic here?).

Regardless of whether you aren't sure precisely what's behind your disgust, they can assist you with working through the feeling and investigate positive methods for adapting to it.

6. Shock

This is another of the fundamental sorts of human emotions. It is commonly short, and we can portray shock by a physiological frighten reaction because of unforeseen things. Shock can be negative, positive, or impartial. The horrendous amazement may include somebody terrifying you as you walk. A case of a charming shock is the point at which you show up home and discover your companions assembled to commend your birthday. We can portray shock by outward appearances, for example, extending the eyes, raising the temples, and opening the mouth. We can likewise describe shock through physical reactions, for example, bouncing up or back and verbal responses, for example, wheezing, shouting, and hollering. Positive surprises to representatives in an association can build their profitability.

Assembling everything

Emotions can be confounded. Some may feel exceptional, while others appear to be mellow in correlation. You may feel clashing emotions at some random time.

In any case, emotions can fill a need, in any event, when they're negative. Rather than attempting to change the emotions you experience, consider how you respond to them. It's normally the responses that make difficulties, not simply the emotions.

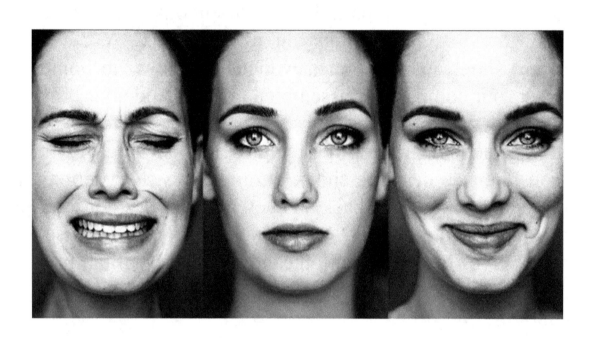

UNDERSTANDING YOUR EMOTIONS

Numerous people feel terrible consistently without knowing why.

A few people are not content with their lives, yet they don't comprehend the purpose of such a feeling.

A great many people get undesirable emotions that they don't see once in a while.

Assume that a little child was crying since it expected to change its garments. In the event that you misjudged the infant's emotions, you may imagine that it's hungry, thus bring it nourishment.

Unquestionably the infant's emotions won't change since you haven't reacted to its genuine interest. That is the equivalent precisely what happens to people when they neglect to comprehend their emotions.

An individual may be encountering emotional agony in view of a problem in his public activity, yet you discover him saying that he is exhausted and that he needs a change. The person goes for that change at that point returns back to locate his awful emotions hanging tight for him by and by. (See Dealing with fatigue)

That is the reason it's critical to comprehend your emotions, and that is the reason you have to comprehend emotional necessities and the explanations for emotional torment.

Emotions are consistent with us. You may feel happy when you snicker with a dear companion or fear when you approach a snarling hound. In any case, there's a whole other world to emotions than simply an abstract understanding of them. You can likewise figure out how to comprehend your emotions. As of late, researchers have expanded our insight into the idea of emotions—about how various emotions appeared, how emotions control our conduct, and how various emotions sway our bodies and minds. Figuring out how to comprehend your emotions is an intriguing undertaking that can help improve your control over both your sentiments and activities.

Comprehend the root of emotions. Emotions are modified reactions molded by development. They allow you to explore your condition in manners that were commonly versatile previously and are frequently still versatile today.

• For model, emotions like fear advanced after some time. At the point when our human precursors, who had the ability to encounter fear, saw a lofty bluff, they carried on more warily as they approached the cliff. Since they played it safe, people who experienced fear were bound to get by than those unafraid. The fearful people lived long enough to recreate and brought forth youngsters with a comparative limit with respect to fear.

• Evolution chose for both negative emotions like fear and positive emotions, for example, happiness. Negative emotions discourage people from activities that are destructive or expensive. Then again, constructive emotions rouse people towards conceivably advantageous activities.

Know the fundamental emotions. Most analysts concur that there are a lot of alleged "fundamental emotions" with which all people are supplied. These essential emotions are anger, disgust, fear, happiness, pity, and shock.

• Many people have extended the rundown of emotions to incorporate disdain, pride, disgrace, love, and nervousness. There might be more fundamental emotions than that. However, the degree to which they are generally experienced or culture-explicit stays begging to be proven wrong.

At the point when you begin putting language on your emotions or partner the name of a feeling with what you're feeling, you start building up your understanding and mindfulness around emotions. You better comprehend what you need or need to do with your sentiments and what is causing them.

Find out about the job emotions play. Emotions are extraordinarily significant for our endurance, our capacity to flourish, and our capacity to use sound judgment. All emotions—even negative ones—assist us with exploring our reality.

• For model, envision, you woke up one day, and you didn't feel humiliated or have any feeling of disgrace or social tension. You, for the most part, couldn't have cared less at all how you acted before others. Odds are you would lose every one of your companions on the off chance that you couldn't have cared less how you acted around them. That is on the grounds that emotions help us to coexist with others.

Perceive how emotions influence dynamics. Emotions are fundamentally critical to our capacity to decide. Emotions offer some incentive or weight to some data along these lines, biasing our dynamic toward some path. People with injuries to parts of their minds that are associated with feeling have disabled dynamic and now and again hindered moral conduct.

• One bunch that experiences difficulty in the public eye is maniacs. One of the key symptomatic basis for psychopathy is an absence of feeling; something many refers to as hard unemotional qualities or absence of empathy or blame. Coming up short on these emotions can prompt introverted and now and then criminal conduct, highlighting the importance of feeling to our feeling of profound quality.

Realize that emotions can get cluttered. Similarly, as you could get a turmoil of your kidneys or eyes, your emotions can likewise get disarranged. In the event that you think your emotions are possibly scattered, converse with psychological well-being proficient about treatment alternatives. A portion of the more typical issue of feeling or mental issue in which emotions are influenced incorporate — discouragement, which includes industrious and enduring sentiments of bitterness and lost intrigue.

• Anxiety issue. General uneasiness issue alludes to broadened and over the top stress over everyday events.

• Schizophrenia can be related to an absence of emotions or a touchy or discouraged state of mind.

• Mania, which for the most part happens in bipolar turmoil, alludes to an all-inclusive time of the anomalous and too much-raised state of mind. Hyper people may likewise be too much and tirelessly fractious.
Record when your emotions happen. When you know when emotions emerge and how they feel, you can take notes on your emotions to additionally get them. To get familiar with the particular emotions you experience and what triggers them in your life, keep a log of when you feel a feeling and record what you think activated it.

• For model, possibly you felt anger, and you reviewed that soon before you understood that you needed to hang tight in line for 15 minutes for lunch, and you despise holding up in lines.

• You can utilize this data to increment or decline the emotions that you need or don't need in your life. On the off chance that you recognize what drives you mad, you can find a way to avoid circumstances that trigger that feeling. For instance, when you realize that you loathe holding up in lines, you can just purchase a little bunch of food supplies one after another, so you can utilize the express path.

Recognizing Your Emotions

Realize what every feeling feels like. People report that various emotions feel diverse emotionally. While the clearest differentiation is that negative emotions feel totally different than positive emotions, diverse negative emotions additionally feel not the same as one another. Humiliation feels not the same as bitterness, which feels not the same as fear.

Realize what anger feels like. Anger is experienced when somebody has wronged you here and there. It serves to prevent them from doing so again later on. Without a feeling like anger, people may more than once exploit you.

The experience of anger once in a while starts in the back between the shoulder bones and ventures upward, along the rear of the neck and around the sides of the jaws and head.

When encountering anger, you may feel hot and bothered.

On the off chance that you notice sensations like strain, torment, and weight in your back, neck, and jaws, you might be disguising your anger.

Realize what disgust feels like. Disgust is a reaction toward horrible improvements, frequently things that can make us genuinely debilitated. It capacities to shield us from things that could make us sick. It can likewise be experienced when we discover things figuratively gross - like certain ethical infringement.

Disgust is felt essentially in the stomach, chest, and head territories of the body. You may really feel wiped out or queasy and end up shutting off your nasal sections and moving endlessly from the repulsive improvements.

Comprehend what fear feels like. Fear is knowledgeable about the reaction to dangerous dangers like bears, statures, or firearms. It causes us to avoid these things at the time and to figure out how to avoid them later on. In spite of the fact that fear is a developed emotional reaction, a considerable lot of the things we fear are found out.

Fear is typically felt fundamentally in the top portion of the body. Notwithstanding, when it includes a fear of statures, fear frequently includes sensation in the legs.

When encountering fear, your heart may pulsate quicker. You may inhale speedier; your palms may feel sweat-soaked and hot as a component of your sensory system gets going. This reaction is the supposed battle or flight reaction.

Realize what happiness feels like. Happiness is knowledgeable about the reaction to things that frequently have ramifications for enduring, flourishing, and passing on one's qualities. Instances of things that fulfill us incorporate having intercourse, having kids, prevailing in an esteemed objective, being lauded by others, and being in a pleasant, inviting condition.

While happiness is maybe one of those most effectively unmistakable or notable emotions, it is likewise one of the hardest to characterize. It can include sentiments of warmth all through the entire body, or it can include a feeling of feeling substance, safe, or enjoy a luxurious lifestyle.

Audit what trouble feels like. Misery is knowledgeable about the reaction to a misfortune that we care about. It is an extremely difficult feeling, which may act to assist us with avoiding misfortunes later on or to acknowledge what we have when we get something back, (for example, on account of a sentimental accomplice).

Trouble regularly starts in the chest and moves upward through the throat and up to the eyes where we see tears. You've likely heard the articulation: "She's completely teared up." Allowing yourself to cry completely can be a purifying encounter. Focusing on the physical sensations in these regions and allowing the vitality to move causes us to lament after misfortune and identify with others' affliction.

Recognize what shock feels like. Shock is experienced when something is startling; however, not esteemed to be a risk. It is an intriguing feeling with regards to that it is generally nonpartisan in valence contrasted with different emotions, which are regularly felt as positive or negative. Shock may capacity to enable re-to arrange thoughtfulness regarding novel unforeseen things.

Shock is felt fundamentally in the head and chest. It is knowledgeable about the reaction to the unforeseen; it can feel like somewhat of a shock.

Before you can comprehend your emotions consummately, you have to comprehend that every individual creates explicit emotional needs at his initial youth that are not the same as the emotional needs others create.

In the event that for a model, the guardians of two kids consistently concentrated on one of them (the most youthful, for instance) at that point, the senior may build up the emotional need of continually needing to be valued and cherished in any event, when he grows up. The more youthful sibling then again may build up the emotional need of needing to be the focal point of consideration since this is the thing that.

At the point when youngsters grow up, they put forth a valiant effort to fulfill their youth emotional requirements, and on the off chance that they didn't figure out how to do so, they experience emotional agony.

For instance, if the senior sibling right now feels increased in value by others when he grew up, then positively he will encounter emotional torment regardless of whether he didn't comprehend the explanation for it.

Step by step instructions to comprehend emotions in the light of emotional needs

You can't comprehend your own emotions until you become mindful of your own emotional needs. At the point when the senior sibling in the past model neglects to locate a caring accomplice, then he may wind up discouraged.

Numerous people scan online for the reasons for discouragement without understanding that 1 million people may be discouraged for 1 million unique reasons. We can comprehend our emotions in a greatly improved manner when we comprehend the way that our mind utilizes them to assist us with accomplishing the emotional needs that are essential to us.

That person constantly needed to be valued, but since he didn't figure out how to do it, his mind reacted with a feeling, for example, misery to spur him to fix the problem.

The other youngster then again may get discouraged in the event that he didn't end up in the focal point of consideration. Again his mind is utilizing such a feeling to rouse him to fulfill his emotional needs.

Understanding emotional agony

Whatever the sort of emotional torment you are encountering, realize that it's only a strategy your mind is utilizing to rouse you to seek after your emotional needs.

On the off chance that your mind found a way that can assist you with fulfilling your emotional needs, then it will inspire you to follow it. A similar inclination the most youthful youngster in the past model will get in the event that he found an opportunity to get celebrated or mainstream.

On the off chance that your mind found that you are moving ceaselessly from your emotional needs, then it will react with emotional agony as misery, terrible temperament, or even discouragement.

Comprehend these realities, and you will have the option to dispose of the entirety of the undesirable emotions in your life.

Emotions like these are a piece of human instinct. They give us data about what we're encountering and assist us in realizing how to respond.

We sense our emotions from the time we're babies. Babies and little youngsters respond to their emotions with outward appearances or with activities like chuckling, snuggling, or crying. They feel and show emotions. However, they don't yet be able to name the feeling or state why they feel that way.

As we grow up, we become progressively gifted in getting emotions. Rather than simply responding as little children do, we can recognize what we feel and put words to it. With time and practice, we show signs of improvement at recognizing what we are feeling and why. This aptitude is called emotional mindfulness.

Emotional mindfulness causes us to recognize what we need and need (or don't need!). It encourages us to fabricate better connections. That is on the grounds that monitoring our emotions can assist us with discussing sentiments all the more obviously, avoid or resolve clashes better, and move past troublesome emotions all the more effectively.

A few people are normally more in contact with their emotions than others. The uplifting news is, everybody can be progressively mindful of their emotions. It just takes practice. Yet, it merits the exertion: Emotional mindfulness is the initial moves toward building emotional intelligence, an ability that can assist people with prevailing in life.

Here are a couple of essential things about emotions:

- Emotions travel every which way. The greater part of us feels a wide range of emotions for the duration of the day. Some last only a couple of moments. Others may wait to turn into a temperament.

- Emotions can be gentle, extraordinary, or anyplace in the middle. The force of a feeling can rely upon the circumstance and on the individual.

- There is nothing more than a bad memory or awful emotions. However, there are acceptable and awful methods for communicating (or following up on) emotions. Figuring out how to communicate emotions in worthy manners is different expertise — overseeing emotions — that is based on the establishment of having the option to get emotions.

It's All Good

A few emotions feel positive — like inclination glad, cherishing, certain, motivated, sprightly, intrigued, appreciative, or included. Different emotions can appear to be increasingly negative — like inclination furious, angry, apprehensive, embarrassed, blameworthy, tragic, or stressed. Both positive and negative emotions are ordinary.

All emotions disclose to us something important to us and our circumstances. In any case, some of the time, we think that its difficult to acknowledge what we feel. We may pass judgment on ourselves for feeling a specific way, as in the event that we feel envious, for instance. Be that as it may, rather than speculation, we shouldn't feel that way, it's smarter to see how we really feel.

Avoiding negative emotions or imagining we don't feel the manner in which we do can blowback. It's harder to move past troublesome emotions and allow them to blur in the event that we don't confront them and attempt to comprehend why we feel that way. You don't need to harp on your emotions or continually talk about how you feel. Emotional mindfulness essentially implies perceiving, regarding, and tolerating your sentiments as they occur.

Building Emotional Awareness

Emotional mindfulness encourages us to know and acknowledge ourselves. So how might you become progressively mindful of your emotions? Start with these three straightforward advances:

1. Make a propensity for checking out how you feel in various circumstances for the duration of the day. You may see that you feel energized in the wake of making arrangements to head off to someplace with a companion. Or then again that you feel apprehensive before a test. You may be loosened up when tuning in to music, propelled by a workmanship display, or satisfied when a companion offers you a commendation. Just notification whatever feeling you feel, at that point name that feeling in your mind. It just takes one moment to do this. However, it's an incredible practice. Notice that every feeling passes and prepares for the following experience.

2. Rate how solid the inclination is. After you notice and name a feeling, make it a stride further: Rate how emphatically you feel the feeling on a size of 1–10, with 1 being the mildest inclination and 10 the most exceptional.

3. Share your emotions with the people nearest to you. This is the ideal approach to work on articulating emotions, an ability that causes us to feel nearer to companions, sweethearts or lady friends, guardians, mentors — anybody.

Make it a day by day practice to impart sentiments to a companion or relative. You could share something that is very close to home or something that is essentially a regular feeling.

Much the same as whatever else in life, with regards to emotions, careful discipline brings about promising results! Remind yourself there is nothing more than a bad memory or awful emotions. Try not to pass judgment on your emotions — simply continue seeing and naming them.

Make the inside outer through craftsmanship. "Emotional workmanship investigation… is an uncommon chance to make the inside, outside

Draw the reaction that rings a bell. Possibly your emotions resemble an image or item or scene or figure. Perhaps it's dynamic. Perhaps it's progressively similar to lines, hues, or shapes. Whatever emerges, sit with it, without judgment.

Keep day by day log of your emotions. Thinking about your emotions consistently. Notwithstanding focusing on what you're feeling, center around what happened to make you feel along these lines. "To what extent did the inclination last? How was it to encounter this feeling?"

Get inquisitive about consideration. People ought to get inquisitive about the message their emotions are sending them about how to all the more likely consideration for themselves and for other people. This is additionally an incredible reminder that no feeling is "acceptable" or "terrible," she said.

As such, consider what your anger, bitterness, nervousness, or delight is attempting to enlighten you concerning how to rehearse caring self-care as well as how to treat others.

You additionally should seriously think about these inquiries "What do I have to leave or relinquish at this time? What do I need a greater amount of at this time? What is the exercise this feeling may be here to encourage me with the goal that I see a greater amount of life's wealth?"

Diary about your anger or trouble. Pick one feeling to investigate, either anger or bitterness, and react to these inquiries. Do I allow myself to encounter this feeling? If not, why? What do I fear may occur if I somehow managed to encounter it? How might I adapt to this inclination?

Investigate how different sources influence your emotions. The importance of taking a gander at the job web-based social networking plays by the way you believe you should feel. "With web-based life, there is this discernment that people are constantly cheerful or that we ought to or should be glad." This implies you may accidentally begin disclosing to yourself that you shouldn't feel agitated or irate or restless, which may lead you to deny your emotions and cover them. Down profound.

Investigate how different sources influence how you feel (or don't feel) your sentiments. How does your folks' perspective on emotions influence your view today? What did they show you emotions? Shouldn't something be said about other significant guardians in your life? As it were, what impacts how you consider emotions, and how you process them? What changes may you have to make?

Understanding our emotions can be intense, in light of the fact that such a large number of us are progressively used to rejecting them. Furthermore, obviously, agonizing emotions are difficult. It's difficult to sit with our uneasiness, particularly in case you're accustomed to busying, however.

However, setting aside the effort to realize our emotions is basic. Emotions "are a piece of our human experience." So truly set aside the effort to realize our emotions is setting aside the effort to know ourselves. Also, isn't that the establishment for everything.

Where do emotions originate from in the cerebrum

Emotions originate from the subliminal mind. So as to comprehend the idea of the subliminal mind, simply think of it as the piece of your cerebrum that deals with all the things that you are not aware of.

While perusing this Ebook, your heart is thumping, and you are breathing, yet you are not deliberately doing these things on the grounds that your intuitive mind is dealing with the procedure.

That is the reason you may out of nowhere experience a feeling that you weren't anticipating. You just become aware of a feeling after the subliminal mind instigates it.

Your subliminal mind assembles the information, sort's realities, decide the appropriate feeling that ought to be activated, and afterward, it sends it to you. That is the reason you, at times, believe that the feeling appears unexpectedly. It's simply that you weren't cognizant when it was being readied.

Where do emotions originate from, the brain science of emotions

What do you, as a rule, do when your cell phone flags low battery? You unquestionably charge it. When you comprehend that emotions are the technique for correspondence between your cognizant and your intuitive mind, you will discover understanding them turning into a simpler undertaking.

Emotions don't appear unexpectedly as certain people accept; however, they are signals sent with a specific reason.

The wellspring of your emotions and getting over undesirable ones

The principle hotspot for awful and undesirable emotions is the unfortunate propensity people educated of disregarding the signs sent to them by their minds.

Back to the cell phone model, what will occur in the event that you didn't charge the telephone? Or then again, what will occur on the off chance that you cleaned it as opposed to charging it?

Absolutely the problem won't be settled, and the equivalent precisely occurs with your emotions when you don't react to the sign.

Rather than asking yourself where do emotions originate from, you ought to solicit yourself what's the reason from these emotions. When you comprehend the reason for a feeling, you will discover the message that your subliminal mind is attempting to let you know, and you will have the option to act in like manner.

In the event that you are feeling on edge, at that point react to that feeling by getting ready yourself much more

In the event that you are discouraged, at that point react to that feeling by bringing back expectation

In the event that you are envious, at that point, react to that feeling by building self-certainty.

The best way to dispose of an undesirable feeling is to comprehend its source, the reason the intuitive mind is attempting to reach and afterward react to it.

HOW TO DEVELOP EMOTIONAL INTELLIGENCE

EMOTIONAL INTELLIGENCE: Emotional intelligence alludes to the capacity of an individual to oversee and control their emotions and has the capacity to control the emotions of others also. As it were, they can impact the emotions of others too.

Emotional intelligence is a significant aptitude in administration. It is said to have five primary components, for example, - self-mindfulness, self-guideline, inspiration, empathy, and social aptitudes.

It additionally implies the ability of people to perceive their own emotions and those of others, observe between various sentiments and mark them properly, utilize emotional data to direct reasoning and conduct, and oversee as well as modify emotions to adjust to conditions or accomplish one's goal(s).

Here is the thing that emotional intelligence additionally implies:

- Agreeableness

- Optimism

- Happiness

- Motivation

- Calmness

While these characteristics are significant, they have little to do with intelligence or emotions, and nothing to do with emotional intelligence.

Emotional intelligence is the ability to reason about emotions and emotional development, and of emotions to upgrade thought.

"Emotional intelligence is the capacity to see emotions; to get to and create emotions to help thought; to get emotions and emotional information, and to brilliantly manage emotions in order to advance emotional and scholarly development."

People who are considered to have high EI can fathom an assortment of feeling related problems precisely and rapidly. They can accurately see emotions in faces in others and what the emotions pass on. For example, they realize that irate people can be dangerous, that upbeat people need to relate with others, and those miserable people frequently like to be distant from everyone else.

High EI people are skilled in dealing with their own just as others' emotions. They realize how to utilize emotional scenes in their own lives to advance explicit sorts of reasoning. Taking care of problems requires less psychological exertion for those high in EI. These people additionally will, in general, be higher in verbal, social, and different intelligence. They are commonly increasingly open and pleasant and are attracted to occupations, including social cooperations, for example, educating, advising, and collaborating with others.

As of late, emotional intelligence – likewise alluded to as EQ is amazingly important that it represents around 60 percent of execution in a wide range of employments. The workplace need never again wait in dimness with respect to the elements prompting extraordinary execution. The more consideration you pay to your own emotional intelligence abilities, the more prominent achievement you will get in your vocation and life. Creating EI will require significant investment, yet will prompt practical conduct changes. By along these lines, you can improve the method for overseeing yourself and the method for working with others. This Ebook will concentrate on some basic parts of emotional intelligence, not all. The tips contained right now pointed for the most part at improving the following arrangement of gifts. Here they are:

Step by step instructions to Develop Emotional Intelligence

1. Comprehend the Role Of Emotional Intelligence (EI)

Most importantly, to improve your emotional intelligence, you have to know its job in everyday life. When you can do that, at that point, attempt to acknowledge how unequivocally supportive and magnificent it is control and assess sentiments, and to ace the likelihood to see. Controlling great the emotions and sentiments will be useful for your vocation as well as for your life and your connections. Regardless of you were not brought into the world with a high emotional intelligence coefficient, you can use in any case practice with a touch of difficult work. From that point onward, you will be progressively satisfied with the outcomes!

2. Self-Awareness

You have to know how your considerations sway your emotions and how your emotions influence your activities. In this way, you would do well to begin from self-mindfulness. This is the way to begin to move your vitality and create EI. At the point when you do anything, simply focus on how you respond to circumstances encompassing and what considerations are experiencing the head when you do it. On the off chance that there is somebody cutting off you out and about, your idea is "the thing that a bonehead," and afterward, you will, in general, become anger. Rather, you can imagine that "stunning, she or he should be very rush to get somebody." As you do this, your feeling would result in all likelihood, positive, and entirely unexpected. When you become self-mindfulness, you can address what triggers your sentiments.

3. Self-Regulation and Self-Evaluation

This is the capacity to control emotions just as motivations. Those people who can self-control don't allow themselves to turn out to be excessively envious and irate. Additionally, they don't settle on reckless and rash choices. Along these lines, you have to think cautiously before making a move so as to set up the attributes of keenness, comfort with change, trustworthiness, and the capacity to state no.

In addition, you have to distinguish your own shortcomings, analyze how you respond to unpleasant circumstances, how your moves sway others, and make obligations regarding your activities. A few people normally imagine that they are phenomenal at everything, and others regularly under-gauge their qualities. This is on the grounds that they are guided by their emotional information that they probably won't know about.

4. Empathy

This is considered as the basic hint on the most proficient method to create emotional intelligence. Empathy is the capacity to perceive and comprehend the requests, needs, and perspectives of those people who are living around you. In the event that you need to turn into an individual who is acceptable at empathy, you have to place yourself in the shoes of others. Everybody sees the world in various and different manners, and everything that individual does and says can bode well from their perspective, yet it sounds good to you. To be a compassionate individual, it is vital for you to recognize the emotions and sentiments of others, even with the sentiments that appear to be unclear. When you control this capacity, you will end up being a compassionate individual and have the option to oversee connections in their profession and life. Practice empathy on companions and friends. All above, you ought not to use generalization and judge others too quickly.

5. Utilize Your Verbal Intelligence To Express Your Thoughts And Feelings

This factor engages recorded as a hard copy, perusing, talking, and bantering. Things being what they are, how you can practice, and build up this angle? By learning a specific new dialect, perusing fascinating books, tuning in to chronicles, utilizing a PC, playing word games, or participating in conversations and discussion on the web, you can upgrade your verbal intelligence. Take a guide to perceive how one of these exercises can assist you with boosting your EI. Learning another dialect implies that you can see the world in another way. There are a few articulations and originations that simply show up in a specific language while don't show up in others.

Realizing how to communicate your sentiments can help you in dealing with your emotions. Obviously, you can. On the off chance that you suppress everything and contract your contemplations and feelings with others, you will make a forlorn life. In this way, simply open your mind and begin sharing your convictions and feeling with people around.

6. Legitimate Intelligence

One of the basic ways on the best way to create emotional intelligence that most specialists prescribe people to unite is legitimate intelligence. This includes perceiving examples and connections, registering and numbering aptitudes courses of events and requests, and the capacity to manage different kinds of problems identifying with rationale. You could practice it by sequencing and arranging exercises, playing rationale and number games, or settling various types of riddles. For example, you can do Sudoku a little every day to improve your coherent intelligence.

.

7. Be Socially Responsible

This is perhaps the highest degree of emotional experience. It represents that you really care about others, particularly those less blessed. There are a few layers of social obligation that rely upon the commitment you provide for other people. You can serve on a board, be a charitable worker, or take an interest in any of various ways. By along these lines, you are expanding your social obligation effectively.

8. Be Open-Minded And Curious

This is one of the most straightforward and least demanding tips on the best way to create emotional intelligence.

That you can apply to help your EI, continually being liberal and inquisitive, will assist you with drawing nearer to other people. Open up to new thoughts as opposed to keeping up a bias which is related to low emotional intelligence. Attempt to nourish your scholarly interest with the reasonable "nourishment." You are going to see positive changes in a matter of seconds.

9. Be Optimistic

On the off chance that you are skeptical, you generally observe everything with trouble and boringness. In opposite, on the off chance that you are an idealistic individual who consistently observes the excellence in all things, you will feel more joyful. This is the aftereffect of a receptive outlook. Consequently, attempt to kill the entirety of the negative contemplations insane and begin taking a shot at hopefulness level from now. Everybody all needs to associate with people with good faith instead of those with negative. Clearly, you won't be a special case. Simply distinguish your characteristics and value them with a glad demeanor. Here are a few different ways that assist you with rehearsing your EI:

- Try to value your great highlights

- Identify the positive qualities in others.

- Make the best out of difficult circumstances.

- Make utilization of hardships as a fuel of advancement.

- Develop the comical inclination and figure out how to see the advantages and lighter side of challenges.

10. Simply Be More Rational

With regards to EI, people ordinarily consider emotions, and in some cases, they over-do everything. Examine your emotions and sentiments, recognize them, and comprehend their causes and their triggers. Anyway, don't over-break down them since you may need to invest a ton of time, exertion, and vitality on it. Continuously attempt to adjust among emotional and objective considerations for controlling your life proficiently.

11. Change Your Mood and Do Something Different

Most of the people ordinarily observe that states of mind are likely a tempest; everything they can do is holding up until they pass. All things considered, dissimilar to climatic tempests that we scarcely transform anything, with the state of mind storm, we can impact, even change the dispositions without expending any unhealthy methods like liquor or medications. One approach to adjust your mind-set is to accomplish something different promptly. In the event that you feel cross, intentionally focus on things in your life for which you can feel thankful. The significant thing is simply to think or accomplish something else in an alternate manner. The best and most quick approach to do this might be basically envisioned not in feeling the manner in which you are feeling. This will, at any rate, balance the awful state of mind and may even set you feeling great. Simply check out it, and you will see the inconceivable outcome in a brief period.

In this way, these were a few hints on the most proficient method to create emotional intelligence. Expectation you have gained some new useful knowledge! All things considered, figuring out how to create emotional intelligence requires a lot of exertion and tolerance, and keeping it straightforward and guiltless is the way to make it fruitful.

On the off chance that you care about the Ebook, we are available to respect any conversation about the theme. Leave your remarks toward the finish of this post to tell us what you think. We value your commitment and will reaction all as quickly as time permits.

Emotional intelligence (EQ) is the capacity to take advantage of your emotions and use them to improve your life. Being in contact with your emotions allows you to oversee feelings of anxiety and discuss effectively with others, two abilities that upgrade your life both by and by and expertly. In contrast to IQ, which stays steady for the duration of your life, EQ can be created and sharpened after some time. See Step 1 to figure out how to build up your emotional intelligence utilizing systems you can attempt immediately.

1. Taking advantage of Your Emotions

Note your emotional responses to occasions for the duration of the day. It's anything but difficult to put your emotions about what you experience for the duration of the day as a second thought. In any case, setting aside some effort to recognize how you feel about encounters is fundamental to improving your EQ. On the off chance that you disregard your sentiments, you're overlooking significant data that bigly affects your mindset and the manner in which you carry on. Begin giving more consideration to your sentiments and associating them to encounters.

For instance, say you're grinding away, and you get cut off during a gathering. What emotions emerge when this occurs? Then again, how would you feel when you get adulated for good work? Getting into the act of naming your emotions as misery, shame, satisfaction, happiness, or some other number of sentiments will begin raising your EQ immediately.

• Get prone to take advantage of your emotions at specific occasions each day. What are your first emotions after waking? Are you last before you nod off?

2. Pay regard for your body. Rather than disregarding the physical indications of your emotions, begin tuning in to them. Our minds and bodies are not separate; they influence each other profoundly. You can raise your EQ by figuring out how to peruse physical signs that educate you on what emotions you're feeling. For model:

• Stress may feel like a bunch in your stomach, tight chest, or speedy relaxing.

• Sadness may want to wake up with slow, substantial appendages.

• Joy, joy, or anxiety may feel like butterflies in your stomach, a hustling heart of expanded vitality.

3. Observe how your emotions and conduct are connected. When you feel compelling emotions, how would you respond? Tune into your gut reactions to circumstances you face each day, rather than simply responding with no reflection. The more you comprehend what spikes your social driving forces, the higher your EQ will be, and you'll have the option to utilize what you know to really change your conduct later on. Here are a few instances of practices and what's behind them:

• Feeling humiliated or uncertain may make you pull back from discussion and detach.

• Feeling irate may make you speak more loudly or furiously storm off.

• Feeling overpowered may make you freeze and forget about what you were doing, or cry.

4. Avoid passing judgment on your own emotions. All the emotions you have are substantial, even the negative ones. On the off chance that you judge your emotions, you'll hinder your capacity to completely feel, making it increasingly hard to utilize your emotions in positive manners. Consider it along these lines: each feeling you have is another bit of valuable data associated with something that is going on in your reality. Without this data, you'd be left in obscurity about how to respond sufficiently. That is the reason the capacity to feel your emotions is a type of intelligence.

• It's hard from the outset, yet work on allowing negative emotions to emotions and associating them with what's going on. For instance, on the off chance that you feel harshly jealous, what is that feeling enlightening you regarding your circumstance?

• Fully experience positive emotions, as well. Associate your happiness or fulfillment to what's going on around you, so you can figure out how to feel them all the more regularly.

5. Notice examples in your emotional history. It's another method to learn as much as you can about your own sentiments and how they're associated with your encounters. At the point when you have a compelling feeling, ask yourself when you last felt like this. What occurred previously, during, and after?
• When you see designs, you can apply more control over your conduct. See how you dealt with a specific circumstance previously, and how you'd prefer to deal with it next time.

• Keep a diary of your emotional responses, or how you feel from every day, so you can obviously perceive how you will get in general respond.

6. Practice concluding how to act. You can't help what emotions you feel. However, you can remain associated with something that is occurring in your reality. Without this data, you would be left in obscurity about how to enough to respond. That is the reason the capacity to feel your emotions is a type of intelligence.

• It's hard from the outset; however, work on allowing negative emotions to emotions and interfacing them to what's going on. For instance, in the event that you feel harshly desirous, what is that feeling enlightening you concerning your circumstance?

• Fully experience positive emotions, as well. Interface your bliss or fulfillment to what's going on around you, so you can figure out how to feel that all the more regularly.

Work on concluding how to carry on. You can't help what emotions you feel, yet you can choose how you need to respond to them. On the off chance that you have an issue with lashing out in anger or closing down when you're harmed, consider how you'd preferably respond. Rather than letting your emotions overpower you, conclude how you will carry on next time your sentiments become solid.

• When something negative occurs in your life, pause for a minute to feel your emotions. A few people portray it as having a flood of bitterness or anger wash over them. When the underlying wave has passed, settle on a choice about how you need to carry on. Choose to impart your sentiments as opposed to curbing them, or find a workable pace again as opposed to quitting.

• Don't go to idealist propensities. It is difficult to let terrible emotions completely ascend to the surface, and numerous people pack them somewhere near drinking excessively, watching a great deal of TV, or going to different propensities that unresponsive the agony. Do this frequently enough, and your EQ will start to endure.

For what reason would it be advisable for you to attempt to encounter your negative emotions notwithstanding your positive ones completely?

To figure out how to control the physical appearances of your emotions.

So you can figure out how to stifle them.

To rebuff yourself

So you can decide their importance.

Interfacing With Other People

1. Be receptive and pleasing. Receptiveness and being pleasant go connected at the hip with regards to emotional intelligence. An

intolerance is commonly a sign of a lower EQ. At the point when your mind is open through understanding and inner reflection, it gets simpler to manage clashes in a quiet and self-guaranteed way. You will get yourself socially mindful, and new conceivable outcomes will be available to you. To reinforce this component of your EQ, consider:

• Listening to banters on TV or the radio. Think about the two sides of the contention, and search for the nuances that require nearer assessment.

• When somebody doesn't respond emotionally to a similar way, you would, consider why this is, and attempt to see it from their perspective.

2. Improve your empathy abilities. Empathy implies having the option to perceive how others are feeling and offer emotions with them. Being a progressively attentive person and truly focusing on what people are stating can assist you with showing signs of improvement feeling of how they're feeling. At the point when you can utilize that data to illuminate your choices and improve your connections, that is an indication of emotional intelligence.

• To improve empathy, come at the situation from others' perspectives. Consider how you would feel on the off chance that you were in their circumstance. Effectively envision how it must be to experience the encounters they're having and what may ease a portion of their hardship as far as to help and care.

• When you see somebody experience a compelling feeling, ask yourself, "How might I respond in a similar circumstance?"

• Be really inspired by what people are stating, so you can respond in a touchy way. Rather than allowing your musings to thoughts, pose inquiries and abridge what they're stating, so it's reasonable you're in the discussion.

3. Read people's non-verbal communication. Try attempting to figure out the real story and get on people's actual emotions by watching their outward appearances and other non-verbal communication. Frequently people say one thing when the expression all over uncovers that there's a more profound truth. Work on being increasingly attentive and getting on the more subtle ways that people impart their emotions.

• If you don't know what you're talented at deciphering outward appearances, take a stab at taking a test to tell. A higher manner of speaking demonstrates that somebody's focused.

4. See the impact you have on others. Understanding others' emotions is just a large portion of the fight with regards to EQ; you additionally need to comprehend the impact you're having on others. Do you will, in general, cause people to feel apprehensive, merry, or furious? What befalls discussion when you stroll in the room?

• Think about what designs you may need to change. In the event that you will provoke your friends and family, your sweetheart cries effectively during discussions, or people will come in general close up a piece when you come around, you may need to change your demeanor with the goal that you have a superior emotional impact on people.

• Ask confided in companions or friends and family their opinion of your emotionality where you have space for improvement.[4]

• An individual's manner of speaking can likewise be of effect. You may experience difficulty perceiving the impact you have on others, and they can help.

5. Practice being emotionally legit. On the off chance that you state you're "fine" and have a glare all over, you're not imparting sincerely. Work on being all the more truly open with your emotions, so people can peruse you better. Tell people when you're disturbed, and share happiness and satisfaction also.

• Being "yourself" helps others truly find a good pace, and they'll confide in you more on the off chance that they see where you're coming from.

• However, comprehend that there's a line: control your emotions so as not to hurt others with them.

•

How might you improve your empathy aptitudes?

Be emotionally legitimate

Decline your pressure

Come to the situation from someone else's perspective.

Think regularly

Putting EQ to Practical Use

1. See where you have the opportunity to get better. Being mentally skilled is significant in life; however, being emotionally smart is similarly as basic. Having high emotional intelligence can prompt better connections and openings for work. There are four center components to emotional intelligence that assist you with having a fair existence. Peruse this and choose where you may have the opportunity to get better, at that point find a way to rehearse your aptitudes around there:

- Self mindfulness: The capacity to perceive the truth about your own emotions and comprehend their sources. Self-mindfulness implies knowing your qualities and restrictions.

- Self the board: The capacity to postpone satisfaction, balance your requirements with those of others, step up, and to pull back on impulsivity. Self-administration implies having the option to adapt to change and to remain submitted.

- Social mindfulness: The capacity to be receptive to others' emotions and worries, just as having the option to notice and adjust to meaningful gestures. Being socially mindful methods having the option to see the force elements at play inside any gathering or in a hierarchical setting.

- The relationship the board: The capacity to coexist well with others, oversee strife, move and impact people and to impart unmistakably.

2. Lower your feeling of anxiety by raising your EQ. Stress is a catchall word for feeling overpowered by a wide range of emotions. Life is loaded up with troublesome circumstances from relationship breakdowns to work misfortune. In the middle of, there are bunch pressure triggers that can make any day by day issue appear to be considerably more testing than it presumably is. In case you're focused on a great deal, it's hard to carry on in the manner in which you need to. Having a decent arrangement for easing pressure improves all parts of your EQ.

- Figure out what triggers your pressure, and what soothes it. Make a rundown of effective types of pressure alleviation, such as spending time with a companion or going for a stroll in the forested areas, and set out to really utilize it.

- Get help on the off chance that you need it. On the off chance that your pressure feels too overpowering to even think about dealing with alone, look for the assistance of a specialist or clinician who can give you devises to adapt (and assist you with bringing your EQ up all the while).

3. Be all the more carefree at home and at work.[6] When you're idealistic, it's simpler to see the excellence in life and ordinary items and spread that feeling to people around you. Confidence brings about emotional prosperity and more prominent changes – people need to be around a hopeful individual, and this attracts

them to you, with all the potential outcomes that more associations bring you.

• Negativity urges people to concentrate just on what can turn out badly as opposed to building flexibility.

• People with high EQ will participate in general ability to utilize fun and cleverness to cause themselves as well as other people to feel more secure and more joyful. Use giggling to overcome intense occasions.

The Signs of Low Emotional Intelligence

Low emotional intelligence is a problem that can have an impact on a wide assortment of social connections. A few specialists even recommend that emotional intelligence may really be a higher priority than IQ in deciding in general achievement in life.

Consider the last time you got into a contention with another person since they didn't see how you felt. Or then again consider the last time you had strife with someone else in light of the fact that you couldn't comprehend what they were feeling. In the two cases, emotional intelligence may assume a job in the hidden clash.

Emotional intelligence can assume a significant job, by the way, we interface with others.1 Sometimes associates, businesses, companions, relatives, and different colleagues may battle with poor emotional abilities that make social circumstances troublesome and full of strain. In different cases, it may even be your own emotional intelligence abilities that need a little work.

A person's degree of emotional intelligence is regularly alluded to as their emotional intelligence remainder or EQ. Here is a portion of the great indications of low emotional intelligence.

1. Getting in Lots of Arguments

You most likely know somebody who consistently appears to get into contentions with others. Companions, family, collaborators, and even irregular strangers wind up entangled in debates with these pugnacious people. Since low EQ people battle to comprehend the emotions of others, they regularly get themselves contending without thinking about how others are feeling.

2. Not Understanding How Others Feel

Low EQ people are frequently totally negligent of the sentiments of others. They don't understand that their life partners may resent them or that their collaborators are aggravated. That as well as feeling extremely irritated that others anticipate that they should know how they are feeling. Emotions, when all is said in done, will, in general, irritate people with low EQ.

3. Thinking That Other People Are Overly Sensitive

People who are low in EQ may break off jokes at unseemly occasions. For instance, they may make a joke at a memorial service or just after a deplorable occasion. At the point when others respond to such off the mark jokes, the low EQ individual may feel like others are just being excessively touchy. These people experience issues understanding the emotions of others, so it's a little miracle why they can't decipher the emotional tone after such occasions.

4. Refusing to Listen to Other Points of View

Low EQ people feel that they are correct and will shield their situation with extraordinary power, yet decline to tune in to what others need to state. This is especially valid if others are disparaging of how the individual doesn't comprehend what others are feeling. They are frequently cynical and excessively disparaging of others' sentiments.

5. Blaming Others for Mistakes

People with low emotional intelligence have little understanding of how their own emotions may prompt problems. At the point when things turn out badly, their first sense is at fault others. They regularly accuse attributes of the circumstance or the practices of others for their activities. They may recommend that they had no other decision for what they did and that others are just not understanding their circumstance. This inclination to not assume liability regularly leaves them feeling severe and deceived.

6. An Inability to Cope With Emotionally-Charged Situations

Forceful emotions, regardless of whether their own or those of others are hard to appreciate for those with low emotional intelligence. These people will frequently leave such circumstances to avoid managing the emotional aftermath. Concealing their actual emotions from others is additionally normal.

7. Sudden Emotional Outbursts

The capacity to control emotions is one of the five basic parts of emotional intelligence. People with low EQ frequently battle to comprehend and control their emotions. They may have sudden emotional upheavals that appear to be overblown and uncontrollable.

8. Difficulty Maintaining Friendships

Since low EQ people frequently put on a show of being rough and pitiless, they experience issues looking after companionships. Dear companionships require a common give-and-take, sharing of emotions, empathy, and emotional help, all of which low EQ people battle with.

9. Lack of Empathy

Since people with low emotional intelligence don't comprehend the emotions of others, they experience little empathy for others. They don't get what others are feeling, so it is unimaginable for them to put themselves from someone else's perspective.

Poor emotional intelligence can unleash destruction in different territories of an individual's life. School, work, family, companionships, and sentimental connections are only a couple of regions where an individual with low EQ will experience serious problems.

Habits of Emotionally Intelligent People

"Anybody can lose control—that is simple. Yet, to be furious with the perfect individual, to the correct degree, at the opportune time, for the correct reason, and in the correct way—that isn't simple."

Emotionally astute people take part in various propensities and practices that add to their capacity to deal with their own emotions and comprehend the sentiments of others. Do you know any individual who is definitely sensitive to their own sentiments, equipped for communicating emotions in a fitting way, just as compassionate and comprehension of how others are feeling? That individual is presumably an emotionally wise person.

Emotional intelligence includes four significant aptitudes:

- The capacity to see emotions.

- The capacity to prevail upon emotions.

- The capacity to get emotions.

- The capacity to oversee emotions.

Look at these key things that emotionally canny people do so you can attempt to make a portion of these a propensity in your own everyday life. Also, take this test to decide how emotionally smart you are, the appropriate response may shock you! You can likewise look at being a low, emotionally insightful individual.

1. Emotionally insightful people focus on what they are feeling.

Self-mindfulness is one of the key segments of emotional intelligence. Self-mindfulness includes the capacity to perceive states of mind, emotions, and sentiments. Some portion of self-mindfulness additionally includes monitoring how your emotions and states of mind impact others. This capacity to screen your own emotional states is a fundamental necessity for emotional intelligence.

2. They see how others feel.

Empathy is another of Goleman's significant components of emotional intelligence. This includes the capacity to comprehend the emotions of others. So as to cooperate with others in numerous living spaces, for example, at work or at school, you should have the option to realize what they are feeling. On the off chance that a collaborator is disturbed or disappointed, realizing what he is feeling can give you a greatly improved thought of how to react.

3. They can manage their emotions.

Self-guideline is totally vital to emotional intelligence. Understanding your emotions is extraordinary, yet not especially valuable on the off chance that you can't utilize this information. Emotionally shrewd people think before they follow up on their sentiments. They are in line with how they feel, yet they don't let their emotions rule their lives.

4. They are roused.

Emotionally shrewd people are spurred to accomplish their objectives and fit for dealing with their practices and sentiments so as to make long haul progress. They may be anxious about rolling out an improvement in their lives. However, they realize that dealing with this fear is significant. By taking a jump and rolling out the improvement, they realize that they may improve their lives and come one bit nearer to achieving their objectives.

5. They have incredible social aptitudes.

Emotionally wise people likewise will, in general, have solid social abilities, presumably to some degree since they are so receptive to their own sentiments just as those of others. They realize how to manage people effectively, and they have put resources into keeping up healthy social connections and aiding everyone around them succeed.

6. They are willing and ready to talk about emotions with others.

Now and then, people are sympathetic and in line with their emotions, however, a battle to really impart these sentiments to other people. Emotionally astute people do not just get sentiments; they realize how to communicate them properly.

What precisely do we mean by properly? Envision, for instance, that you simply had an especially horrendous day at work. You are worn out, disappointed, and furious about how things went at a significant gathering. An improper articulation of your emotions may include returning home and getting into contention with your mate or sending an awful email to your chief. A progressively suitable emotional response would talk about your dissatisfactions with your life partner, discharging some pressure by going for a run and concocting an arrangement to improve the following day than the one preceding.

7. They can effectively recognize the basic reasons for their emotions.

Envision that you wind up getting baffled and furious with a collaborator. As you evaluate your sentiments, break down what you're truly disturbed about. It is safe to say that you are frantic about your associate's activities, or does your anger come from basic disappointments and weight from a supervisor who has stacked an excessive amount of work and obligation on your shoulders? Emotionally insightful people can take a gander at the circumstance and accurately recognize the genuine wellspring of their sentiments.

From the start, this may appear to be a simple errand; however, actually, our emotional lives can be both entangled and chaotic. Finding the specific wellspring of your sentiments can be especially dubious when you are managing ground-breaking emotions, for example, love and anger.

How to Increase Your Social Intelligence

People with social intelligence can detect how others feel, know naturally what to state in social circumstances, and appear to be self-guaranteed, even in a bigger group. You may think about these societies as having "people aptitudes," yet what they really have is social intelligence.

Indications of Social Intelligence

People who are socially smart presentation center qualities that assist them with conveying and interface with others.

- Effective Listening: An individual who has social intelligence doesn't listen only to react, rather focusing on what someone is saying.

- Conversational Skills: Some people have conversational aptitudes that empower them to carry on a conversation with for all intents and purposes anyone. They're careful, fitting, clever, and earnest in these discussions, and they recall insights concerning people that allow the exchange to be progressively important.

- Reputation Management: Socially smart people consider the feeling that they make on others. Thought about one of the most mind-boggling components of social intelligence, dealing with notoriety requires cautious parity—an individual should attentively make an impact on someone else while as yet being valid.

- Lack of Arguing: Someone with social intelligence comprehends that contending or demonstrating a point by causing someone else to feel terrible isn't the best approach. They don't through and through reject someone else's thoughts, yet rather hear them out with a receptive outlook—in any event, when it is anything but thought that they actually concur with.

The most effective method to Develop Social Intelligence

While a few people may appear to create social intelligence without truly trying, others need to work to create it. Fortunately, certain procedures can enable an individual to assemble social abilities. These strategies can assist you in creating social intelligence:

- Pay close regard for what (and who) is around you. Socially savvy people are perceptive and focus on unpretentious expressive gestures from everyone around them. In the event that you believe that somebody in your life has resilient people aptitudes, observe how they associate with others.

- Work on expanding your emotional intelligence. Albeit like social intelligence, emotional intelligence is increasingly about how you control your own emotions and how you feel for other people. It requires perceiving when you're encountering a feeling—which will assist you with perceiving that feeling in others—and managing them suitably. An emotionally wise individual can perceive and control negative sentiments, for example, dissatisfaction or anger, when in a social setting.

- Respect social differences. Many people take in people's abilities from their family, companions, and the network is encompassing them, a socially astute individual comprehends that others may have various reactions and customs dependent on their childhood.

- Practice undivided attention. Build up your social intelligence by taking a shot at your relational abilities—which requires undivided attention. Try not to intrude. Set aside an effort to consider what another person is stating before you react. Tune in to the emphases in what others state, which can give you intimations to what they truly mean.

- Appreciate the notable people in your life. Socially astute people have profound associations with people who are significant to them. Focus on the emotions of your life partner and kids, companions, associates, and different friends. In the event that you overlook the nearest people in your life, you're feeling the loss of the signals on the most proficient method to associate with them.

Utilizing Emotional Intelligence in the Workplace

Emotional intelligence, at times alluded to as EQ ("emotional remainder"), alludes to an individual's capacity to perceive, comprehend, oversee, and reason with emotions. It is a basic capacity with regards to relational correspondence—and an intriguing issue in brain science as well as in the business world.

The term itself was authored by therapists during the 1990s, yet its utilization immediately spread into different regions, including business, instruction, and mainstream society.

Why EQ Is Important for Success

The idea immediately grabbed the eye of the general population, including human asset chiefs and business pioneers. Analysts have proposed that emotional intelligence impacts how well representatives interface with their partners. EQ is likewise thought to assume a job in how laborers oversee pressure and struggle just as general execution at work.

Studies have indicated that representatives with higher scores on proportions of EQ additionally will, in general, be evaluated higher on proportions of relational working, authority capacities, and stress the board.

While customary intelligence was a quality-related with initiative achievement, only it was insufficient. People who are effective at work aren't simply brilliant—they additionally have a solid measure of emotional intelligence.

In the event that you need to prevail in the workplace and climb the vocation stepping stool, emotional intelligence is basic to your prosperity.

Why EQ Matters in the Workplace

So for what reason is emotional intelligence such an esteemed workplace ability? As per one overview of procuring chiefs, just about 75 percent of respondents recommended that they esteemed a representative's EQ more than their IQ.

Emotional intelligence is broadly perceived as a significant ability that improves correspondence, the executives, problem-illuminating, and connections inside the workplace. It is additionally expertise that analysts accept can be improved with preparing and practice.

High EQ in the Workplace

- Making better choices and taking care of problems

- Keeping cool under tension

- Resolving clashes

- Having more prominent empathy

- Listening, reflecting, and reacting to productive analysis

Low EQ in the Workplace

- Playing the job of the person in question or not assuming individual liability for mistakes.

- Having detached or forceful correspondence styles

- Refusing to function as a group

- Being excessively incredulous of others or not open to others' sentiments

Step by step instructions to Become More Emotionally Intelligent

While emotional aptitudes may work out easily for certain people, there are things that anybody can do to help improve their capacity to comprehend and prevail upon emotions. This can be especially useful in the workplace, where connections and business choices regularly depend on the relational getting, cooperation, and correspondence.

Factors, for example, childhood and character, will, in general, assume a huge job in the advancement of emotional intelligence. However, it is an ability that can be improved with exertion and practice.

The key emotional abilities not just indicated enduring upgrades in emotional intelligence, they additionally experienced enhancements in physical and mental prosperity, better social connections, and lower cortisol (stress hormone) levels.

So in the event that you are keen on improving your emotional intelligence abilities to profit your workplace execution, there are a couple of things you can do.

5 Categories of Emotional Intelligence

1. Self-mindfulness

2. Self-guideline

3. Social abilities

4. Empathy

5. Motivation

Become More Self-Aware

One of the initial moves toward using emotional intelligence aptitudes in the workplace is to work on perceiving your own emotions. Self-mindfulness includes monitoring various parts of yourself, including your emotions and sentiments. It is one of the primary parts of emotional intelligence.

So as to perceive your emotions and comprehend what is causing these sentiments, you have to act naturally mindful initially.

Focus on How Your Feeling

How do these emotions impact how you react? Do the things you are feeling affect the choices you make or how you associate with others? As you invest more energy thinking about these inquiries, you may find that you become significantly more mindful of your own emotions and the job that they play in your day by day life.

Check out Emotional Strengths and Weaknesses

How well do you speak with others? Do you end up encountering eagerness, anger, or irritation regularly? What are a few different ways you can manage these sentiments effectively? Perceiving your shortcomings allows you to search for approaches to manage such weaknesses.

Recollect That Emotions Are Fleeting

A collaborator may aggravate you, or your supervisor may give you a baffling assignment to finish. Before you respond, recall that these things are brief, so settling on careless choices dependent on extraordinary emotions can be negative to your long haul objectives and achievement.

Practice Self-Regulation

Self-guideline as a basic piece of emotional intelligence. Monitoring your emotions is an important step.

People who have great self-guideline can adjust well to evolving circumstances. They don't contain things. However, they do trust that proper ways will communicate their emotions as opposed to simply responding rashly right now.

They additionally consider how their emotional articulations influence others. Approaches to begin improving your self-guideline aptitudes in the workplace:

- Find procedures to discharge workplace stress. Having leisure activities outside of work is an extraordinary spot to begin. Physical exercise is likewise a healthy method to discharge pressure.

- Keep your cool. Acknowledge the way that you can't control everything, except search for supportive ways that you can reach that don't fan the fire.

- Think before deciding. Emotions can overpower you without giving it much thought. However, you can make a more settled, increasingly normal decision on the off chance that you give yourself a touch of time to think about the entirety of the conceivable outcomes.

Improve Your Social Skills

Emotional people with high EQs likewise have solid social abilities. Since they are adroit at perceiving others' emotions, they can react suitably to the circumstance. Social aptitudes are additionally highly esteemed in the workplace since they lead to a better correspondence and by and large organization culture.

Workers and pioneers with extraordinary social aptitudes can manufacture affinity with partners and convey their thoughts effectively. People with great social abilities are incredibly cooperative individuals. However, they are additionally ready to take on positions of authority when required.

Tune in to What Others Have to Say

This doesn't mean just inactively tuning in to others talk. This doesn't mean just idly checking out others talk. Centered consideration incorporates showing thought, presenting requests, and giving info. Whether or not you are in an organization work or an associate, centered consideration can show that you are lively about work exercises and prepared to work with others to empower the social occasion to land at its destinations.

Concentrate on Nonverbal Communication

The signs that individuals send through their non-verbal correspondence can pass on a lot about what they genuinely think.

Hone Your Persuasion Skills

Having the choice to pass on sway in the work environment and convince partners and executives to check out your contemplations can go far in moving your calling.

Stay away from Office Drama

Give a valiant exertion to stay away from the unimportant working environment gives that once in a while expect power over the work environment, in any case, realize that disputes are not continually avoidable. Focus on slanting to what others have to state and look for ways to deal with deal with issues and farthest point strains.

Become More Empathetic

Genuinely adroit individuals are satisfactory at wandering into another person's perspective and perceiving how they feel. Sympathy is something past seeing how others are feeling, it in like manner incorporates how you respond to these feelings.

In the working environment, sympathy permits you to appreciate the different components among accomplices and directors. It moreover permits you to see who holds power and how it impacts the practices, feelings, and coordinated efforts that stream from such associations.

See Things From the Other Person's Point of View

It will in general be taking a stab at event, especially in case you feel like the other individual isn't right. However as opposed to let contrasts join up with noteworthy conflicts, contribute vitality looking condition from another's perspective. It might be a phenomenal beginning advance toward finding a middle ground between two limiting points of view.

Concentrate on How You Respond to Others

Do you let them get a chance to share their musings? Do you perceive their information, whether or not you restrict this thought? Telling others that their undertakings have merit normally helps everyone with feeling even more prepared to settle.

Work on Your Motivation

Another key part of emotional intelligence is something known as inborn inspiration.

People who have solid EQ will, in general, be progressively persuaded to accomplish objectives for the wellbeing of their own. As opposed to looking for outer prizes, they need to do things since they discover them satisfying, and they are enthusiastic about what they do.

Cash, status, and approval are extraordinary. However, people who are highly fruitful in the workplace are typically inspired by something more than that. They are enthusiastic about what they do. They have a pledge to their work, they love taking on new difficulties, and their energy can appear to be infectious. They don't surrender notwithstanding deterrents, and they can rouse others to try sincerely and endure so as to accomplish objectives.

Concentrate on What You Love About Your Work

Regardless of how you feel about your activity, there are likely going to be things about it that you love and things about it that you loathe. So as to manufacture your inherent inspiration, give centering a shot the parts of your activity that you really appreciate.

Maybe you love the sentiment of achievement you get when you complete a major task. Or then again, perhaps you love helping your customers accomplish progress toward their own objectives. Regardless of what it is, recognize those segments of your activity, and take motivation from them.

Attempt to Maintain a Positive Attitude

Notice how hopeful people in the workplace will, in general, rouse and spur others also. Embracing this sort of demeanor can assist you with feeling all the more emphatically about your work.

Emotional intelligence assumes a significant job in prosperity as well as in your accomplishment in the workplace. Luckily, there are various exercises you can take from feeling brain science that will allow you to improve your EQ and encourage more prominent emotional abilities t to improve your work execution and vocation achievement.

DECLUTTERING YOUR MIND

Decluttering implies less stuff to arrange, yet regularly leaving behind our stuff is more enthusiastically than the greater part of us think. What's more, picking how and what to dispose of can be a mind-boggling task.

Decluttering: Based on the hypothesis that messiness channels, both physical and mental vitality. Decluttering includes two segments. The first spotlights on discharging things (garments, papers, furniture, articles, and thoughts) that never again fill a decent need in one's life. The second spotlights on making a straightforward arrangement of individual association that is anything but difficult to keep up and makes preparations for gathering things that are neither essential nor sustaining.

"Life is as straightforward or confused as we make it."

We as a whole arrangement with it. In some pieces of our reality, we face it: be it in our wardrobes, in our workplaces, or even in our bodies. Be that as it may, the most diverting and weakening jumbled space is in our minds.

At the point when we're up to speed in our minds, occupied by stress or fear, we're absent or perceptive. Also, when we're not perceptive, we lose the association with ourselves, our condition, and our lives.

Mental mess pulls us askew, upsetting our equalization. It can get so cluttered and muddled up there that we end up lost in the fantasy world.

Clearing Clutter at the Root

Be that as it may, a major family will, in general, hold a wide range of messiness. Raised with four kin sharing one washroom, one TV, and one phone allows simply state it got revolting. Likely didn't help that Mom was a shopaholic, and Dad was an accumulator.

The claustrophobia of my youth left me needing to live a mess-free.

It wasn't until my school years from home that I began seeing how my mind was the reason for any messiness I conveyed with me; nothing and nobody else was to be faulted.
After an enormous quarter-life emergency, I perceived how I was trading off my own lucidity and life offset with my own head-garbage—the garbage I kept upstairs.

However, how would you start to gather up the messiness you can't see?

Decluttering the mind expects us to get deliberate on where we place our consideration and how we invest our time and vitality.

Here are a few hints to assist you with doing that.

1. Keep an appreciation log.

Appreciation is acknowledging what you have. It's the maxim that what you have is sufficient. Requiring significant investment consistently to consider your favors will help carry parity to your life. It's difficult to be grateful and irate simultaneously.

Go through five minutes consistently to note in any event five things you're thankful for. A few thoughts: time with a companion, an honor at school, your safety belt, your breath, the hues in the recreation center, and even the supporting magnificence of a blustery day.

2. Diary.

Regardless of whether carefully or with paper, journaling is an awesome arrival of a repressed idea. By recording your contemplations, stresses, expectations, and encounters, you are discovering break from the gab inside your head.

Despite the fact that you're despite everything thinking about these things as you compose, it resembles you're watching the circumstance from ten feet away, never again totally consumed in its emotionality.

Attempt to diary consistently for anyway long it takes to feel tranquility on a subject. The more you do it, the quicker the harmony comes. Like in treatment, basically letting it out is mending since we're assuaged of the weight of keeping everything inside.

3. Chuckle.

Chuckling has been demonstrated to be the best drug for assuaging pressure. It facilitates protectiveness, relieves your emotional burden, and lifts worry off your shoulders. It carries equalization to your mind since giggling is nearness.

Practice not paying attention to yourself so and giggle all the more regularly. Truly giggle. A profound, generous, Santa giggle. Watch comedies, spend time with clever companions, go to a satire club, read the Sunday funny cartoons, or play with your children or your canine. With such a large number of choices, stress doesn't stand an opportunity.

4. Daydream.

Set aside some effort to rest your mind each day. Let your mind shut off from preparing, apply, or decipher data. This implies no TV, no discussion, no perusing, and no problem tackling.

Enjoy a reprieve from the tasks, from the obligations of the day. Allow the breath to go back and forth normally, and the eyes wander any place they need.

Take a gander at the tree's influence, the mists drift, the stars shine. A short time later, when it comes time to work, you'll discover concentrate more effectively than before your small retreat.

5. Control your media admission.

Watching or tuning in to everything without exception since it's on doesn't look good for your mind. Inconspicuous feelings, predispositions, and decisions creep into your mind and install thought structures. Unaware, you at that point structure conclusion that isn't your own, basically in light of the fact that you heard it on the radio.

Start truly focusing on the clamor that you let saturate your eyes and ears. Ask, Is this profiting my life in any capacity?

6. Get imaginative.

As regularly as could be allowed, associate with your internal identity by investigating your creative mind. Allow interest to lead. With regard to changes to get imaginative, there is bounty! A couple of my faves: puzzles, shading, drawing, singing, moving, and in any event, making a supper without any preparation.

The fact of the matter is to become mixed up in stunningness and wonder as you did at five years of age. At the point when you accomplish that feeling from a specific movement, continue doing it!

7. Exercise.

Move. Sweat. Stretch. Get dynamic and get your endorphins moving! Exercise helps control your weight, forestall sickness, support vitality, and improve your state of mind. It encourages you to rest better, feels much improved, and concentrate better.

Discover a movement that motivates you to raise your pulse—move, yoga, hand to hand fighting, running, strolling, whatever. On the off chance that keeps up some degree of incessant action, it will serve your health and prosperity for quite a long time to come.

8. Get clear on your needs.

To make sense of your top needs, list your objectives, your inspirations, and those connections that issue most to you. At that point, rank them arranged by importance to your prosperity. These are the things, individually, that you'll need to invest the most energy in.

Assess whatever interferes with you and your needs—is it worth you settling on what makes a difference most?

9. Accomplish something kind for someone else.

You'll get all that you need in the event that you help other people get what they need." Whatever we feel is inadequate in a circumstance is something we're not giving. Also, whenever we feel the need or aching, we're out of parity.

Sounds outlandish, however in the event that you need to see a greater amount of something in your life, begin parting with that thing—be it love, cash, or consideration.

Make it a point each day to be caring with your activities, your words, and particularly your musings.

On the off chance that you don't feel really moved to loan some assistance or go along a commendation, basically grin. That demonstration alone is sufficient to improve your temperament and clear the psychological blockage among you and empathy.

10. Give up.

Since when does stressing go anyplace? Discharge those pointless, negative contemplations of stress. At the point when we do this routinely, we definitely lessen the measure of "stuff" that needs our consideration and exhausts our vitality.

Drawers and cupboards are by all accounts, not the only zones that need cleaning. Our minds are loaded with considerations as decisions, desires, and fears that visually impaired us from reality. Take a stab at observing your mind and supplanting negative considerations with positive ones. You'll see before long notification an adjustment in your whole point of view.

Keeping up a Balanced Life

Life's brimming with surprises. We control how we react to them, and the most ideal approach to find some kind of harmony is to move with the punches and accept circumstances for what they are. Life's eccentric course is our chance to meet surprises with acknowledgment and elegance.

It assists in having a receptive outlook.

What is the Best Decluttering Method?

We needed an option that is quicker than a multi-month, 3 months, or much more. What's more, 10 minutes per day (always?) simply didn't appear as though it was going to cut it. I realized I had one shot with my significant other to truly make this decluttering procedure effective. She even disclosed to me that she needed to follow the best of the considerable number of approaches and strategies that were out there.

In case you're feeling enclosed by the measure of messiness in your home, similar to me, you've likely gone to the acknowledgment that it's a great opportunity to roll out an improvement.

You have a most likely idea about what life could resemble on the off chance that you recovered your space, making it spotless and composed.

Decluttering implies less stuff to sort out, yet regularly leaving behind our stuff is more diligently than the greater part of us think. Furthermore, picking how and what to dispose of can be a mind-boggling task.

Luckily, there are huge amounts of imaginative decluttering techniques to make the procedure simpler. Top proficient coordinators have created frameworks for separating the procedure and causing it to appear to be increasingly tolerable.

The Benefits of Minimalism: 7 Reasons to Declutter Your Life

"Have nothing in your home that you don't know to be valuable or accept to be wonderful." ~ William Morris

Have you at any point seen that each time you move, you need a greater truck than the last time you moved?

People love to gather things, and we tend to maintain gathering things in control to occupy the accessible space in our homes (and some of the time past).

I'm a firm devotee to the possibility that material belongings don't liken to happiness, so I, as of late, began to investigate carrying on with a moderate lifestyle, to check whether a less jumbled home would bring about a less jumbled mind.

I focused on decluttering every component of my life by diminishing the measure of material belongings I possessed and expelling those that were pointless. This allowed me to concentrate on those things I esteemed most.

I followed the seven stages below to declutter my assets:

Stage 1: Categorized my assets so as to figure out them each in turn (garments, shoes, packs, adornments, beauty care products, gadgets, books, and so forth.)

Stage 2: Gathered together all that I claim from one classification, so I could see the genuine degree of my assets.

Stage 3: Immediately disposed of whatever leaped out at me that I never again required.

Stage 4: Analyzed every single residual thing to distinguish whether I adored them. After cautious thought, I disposed of anything I didn't love or need.

Stage 5: This was where I drove myself to be increasingly savage. I addressed whether I actually really cherished the things in my "keep heap" and evacuated a couple of something else.

Stage 6: Tidied all that I had chosen to keep flawlessly away.

Stage 7: Gave all that I wasn't keeping to companions and good cause shops and sent a few things for reusing.

The way toward evacuating every single material belonging I never again required from my life showed me various exercises:

1.   Mindful buying
We buy numerous things spontaneously, with little thought of need or want. What a misuse of cash to purchase something you may not even especially like!

An exhaustive decluttering session instructs you to be increasingly mindful of a buy and investigate its importance before going through your well-deserved money.

While decluttering my garments, I ran over a few things that, despite everything, had the names joined. I discovered it extremely hard to leave behind these, as it felt so inefficient given that I had never worn them. This was an extraordinary exercise in guaranteeing that starting now and into the foreseeable future, I will just purchase things I am certain I will wear.

2. Cash spared from pointless and trivial buys

Confining buys to just important things has the additional advantage of sparing money. My greatest overspend in the past has been on garments.

3. Time spared by having the option to discover things all the more effectively

Lessening your assets allows you to discover things all the more rapidly, sparing valuable time.

Never again will you need to chase through a reserve of pieces of jewelry yet effectively pick one from the little assortment you have held. No angling around among a heap of purses or establishing through hanger after hanger of garments. The decision is faster and simpler.

4. Space spared from owning less

The fewer belongings you possess, the less extra room you need.

Since doing some genuine decluttering, I presently need a large portion of the space I recently did. I am right now hoping to move to a little condo, as I presently have to an extreme degree an excessive amount of space for one individual and could joyfully live someplace a lot littler.

5. More joyful viewpoint

Encircle yourself with things you love, and showing just the things generally significant to you will cause you to feel more joyful. You won't need to look through loads of things that you don't care for. Most loved things won't get lost at the rear of the organizer or the base of the cabinet.

Gone are the times of sparing your preferred things for an exceptional event. Consistently is an uncommon event since I am just utilizing the things I love, and my life is more joyful thus.

6. Faster and simpler to spotless and clean

The fewer belongings you have, the neater your home will be, and the simpler it will be to keep clean.

This is just conceivable on the off chance that you lessen the measure of your material things. Presently my living space is cleaner and tidier. My mind is less jumbled.

HOW TO IMPROVE RELATIONSHIP

People are social animals, and we flourish in little and medium-sized gatherings. Indeed, even the mavericks out there have a couple of relatives and a few companions in their nearby group of friends. This implies we need to buckle down on growing great associations with people around us—our family, companions, sweethearts, collaborators, and supervisors. Here are a couple of clever little mysteries that will assist you with improving as a people individual and improve any relationship in your life.

One of the most important encounters we can have in our lives is the association we have with other individuals. Positive and steady connections will assist us with feeling healthier, more joyful, and increasingly happy with our lives. Here are a few of tips to assist you with developing increasingly positive and healthy connections in all aspects of your life:

1. Recognize the sentiments, emotions, and requirements of others

It's anything but difficult to become involved with our own little world. Now and then, we feel so anxious to communicate our emotions and perspective that we disregard the sentiments and sentiments of others. On the off chance that you need to fabricate solid, durable connections, you have to begin letting people communicate. Also, consistently regard their entitlement to an assessment, regardless of whether you don't think they are correct.

2. Be increasingly open to recommendations and bargains

Settling on the correct choice and picking a game-plan that benefits everybody requires contribution from everybody included. Attempt to be just when settling on things like where to go for supper or isolating undertakings among associates. Comprehend that you will frequently need to bargain, and this occasionally implies surrendering a ton of ground in another person's kindness.

3. Concentrate on the activity

Carrying out your responsibility as well as can be expected not just improve the connection among you and your associates, it additionally implies not so much pressure but rather more genuine feelings of serenity during your free hours. This will make you not so much crabby but rather more enthusiastic when you spend time with your companions, family, and darling.

4. Invest a greater amount of your free energy out with people rather than bolted up at home

Finding a good pace quality time with your companions, accomplice, and even partners is a basic piece of finding a workable pace on a more profound level. It likewise allows you to unwind and share a wide range of data. Investing more energy outside with others is additionally a decent method to improve your psychological well-being by discussing the problems you may have with your accomplice or companions—problems that would somehow or another destroy you and put a strain on those connections.

5. Take a few to get back some composure on your emotions through standard practice

So as to shield a conversation from growing into contention and to manage the emotional upheavals of others, you should have the option to keep a level head. This implies controlling your emotions. With practices like Bikram yoga, you can get physical health benefits while figuring out how to remain quiet and inhale appropriately. Now and then, a decent run can help clear your head, and discharge contained disappointments.

6. Work on conquering your frailties

In the event that you go into a conversation with somebody and you have huge amounts of weaknesses overloading you, you will consistently be anxious and searching for the best comment. Truth be told, it might be hard for you to open up or meet new people. Invest some energy every day chipping away at dealing with your appearance and lifestyle decisions and begin making some little positive changes. It will significantly improve the manner in which you collaborate with others.

7. Gain proficiency with people's emotional triggers and avoid setting them off

Much the same as you have fears and frailties so does every other person. There are themes and even explicit words that will trigger a solid negative emotional reaction. As you find a workable pace, attempt to get on these unstable subjects, and avoid hitting these triggers when you communicate with that individual. They will extraordinarily value this, and you will battle less frequently.

8. Goodhearted talk is fine, yet keep things positive

Albeit kidding and prodding may not set off any enormous triggers, in the event that you are constantly basic and deriding, people will begin thoroughly considering less of your time. You need people near you to really appreciate your conversation, so make certain to have a healthy parity of exchange and constructive remarks and don't relegate beyond what they can take.

9. Begin saying sorry all the more frequently

Let's be honest, we as whole chaos up some of the time and wind up upsetting a companion, relative, or accomplice. It is critical to acknowledge the fault and state that you are heartbroken. A straightforward "I'm heartbroken" can go far towards keeping up great connections and repairing ones that have taken an awful turn.

10. Figure out how to excuse

This one goes hand and hand with expressions of remorse. You can't simply continue requesting absolution from others while holding feelings of resentment and frowning. Of course, you will require some an opportunity to chill, yet you have to allow people to apologize so you can proceed onward. On the off chance that somebody broadens a delivers a motion of harmony, don't slap it away.

Is it accurate to say that you are Reaching Your Full Potential?

Take Life hack's life potential evaluation and get a custom report dependent on your one of a kind qualities, and find how to begin carrying on with your full life and arrive at your maximum capacity. It's a FREE appraisal!

11. Free yourself from the emotional stuff

This point expands on the past one. Some of the time, people won't move toward you for détente dealings or even say they are upset for something terrible they have done. You don't have to twist around in reverse to revive broke kinships and connections, however, attempt to relinquish such emotional things, let your injuries recuperate and prop up forward without being angry and reprimanding others for every one of your problems.

12. Energize healthy conversations rather than battles

Significant issues will regularly come up, and you should address them with your life partner or your companions and colleagues. This is typical, yet a shouting match where everybody is humiliated will just deplete your vitality. Rather, have a go at remaining quiet. This is the place all that meditation and yoga breathing becomes possibly the most important factor, and talk about your issues without raising your voice or intruding on one another.

13. Quit perspiring the little things

Little issues ought to never at any point find a good pace and problem-explaining stage. On the off chance that it is a generous issue, at that point, simply drop it and never think back. It might irritate you for some time, yet you'll before long overlook it, and it will spare you minutes or long periods of belligerence.

14. Quit thinking about things literally

Not all that somebody says is a hidden affront or astute implication coordinated at you. People don't generally have some profound and shrouded implications in mind, nor are they continually plotting to accomplish a vile objective. Quiet your negative inward voice down and fully trust things without making colossal legitimate jumps dependent on inadequate data. This will cause you to appear to be progressively loose and mindful, and assist you with avoiding humiliating mistaken assumptions and enormous battles about nothing.

15. Try not to make a hasty judgment

Being mindful and suspicious are profoundly established in human instinct. However, some of the time, people go route over the edge with crazy hypotheses and play out situations in their minds that lone serve to chafe them and become angry of someone else who might not have even done anything incorrectly. Try not to let desire, anger, or your weaknesses cloud your judgment and spotlight on progressively effective correspondence that encourages trust.

Listening is pivotal expertise in boosting someone else's self-esteem, the quiet type of sweet talk that causes people to feel bolstered and esteemed.

Dynamic or intelligent listening is the absolute generally valuable and significant listening expertise. In undivided attention, we likewise are truly keen on understanding what the other individual is thinking, feeling, needing, or what the message means, and we are dynamic in looking at our comprehension before we react with our own new message. This check or input process is the thing that recognizes undivided attention and makes it effective.

16. Pose more inquiries and focus when somebody addresses you

By just sitting an individual down, saying what's on your mind and asking them what you need to realize will assist you with avoiding a lot of problems. Likewise, when somebody needs to converse with you, set aside the effort to close your mouth and tune in to what they need to state. Take mental notes and pose inquiries a short time later. This is the key to effective correspondence and building a solid bond between two people.

Offering time to people is additionally an enormous blessing. In reality, as we know it where time is of the pith, and we are attempting to fit in more than one lifetime, we don't generally have the opportunity to provide for our friends and family, companions, and work associates. Innovation has fairly disintegrated our capacity to construct genuine affinity, and we endeavor to perform various tasks by messaging and talking simultaneously.

Being available in the time you provide for people is likewise significant, so that, when you are with somebody, you are genuine with somebody and not choosing to move on or stressing over what's to come. The association we make with others is the very touchstone of our reality, and giving time, vitality, and exertion to creating and building connections is one of the most significant life abilities.

17. Make analysis valuable

At the point when you need to call attention to certain imperfections in an individual's presentation, endeavor to give them input rather than simply condemning, i.e., mention to them what they can do to improve. You ought to likewise toss in little commendations to numb the impacts of analysis. With regards to accomplices, revealing to them you like something that they do will regularly persuade them to rehearse, improve, and improve.

18. Invest some energy with your family in genuinely customary interims

So as to keep your relationship solid, you have to really invest energy with people. The family frequently takes a rearward sitting arrangement to different commitments. However, you should make an opportunity to see your folks, visit family members, or invest quality energy with your accomplice and children. Ensure you give a few quality hours to the people you love in any event once every week for your atomic and once per month for your more distant family. You can generally simply call and have a talk.

19. In case you're a man, "She is in every case right" is the brilliant relationship rule

Ladies typically will, in general, take firm positions on certain things, and on a cultural level, it is satisfactory for them to be progressively emotional and assume responsibility with regards to running the home. Men are relied upon to be more settled and can spare themselves a great deal of difficulty by simply admitting to the lady that she is correct. Obviously, you should make some noise on significant issues and draw a few lines, however, don't attempt to utilize rationale to demonstrate that you are correct – you remain to pick up literally nothing from it.

20. In case you're a lady, "He truly doesn't get a few things, cut him a little room to breath" is the brilliant relationship rule

Women have an altogether different perspective than men and are commonly more emotionally determined, natural, and increasingly open to non-verbal communication cues. You don't should be searching for a perplexing purpose behind why a man is acting a specific way – it is generally the most straightforward clarification, and they truly can't get a handle on specific things. Simply cut them a little leeway every once in a while and realize that they truly are making a decent attempt, their minds are simply not wired a similar way.

21. For both same-sex and hetero couples: pick your fights and let your accomplice win every now and then

Regardless of what your sexual inclination or relationship status – in the event that you are in it for the long haul, you'll have to understand that you will, on occasion, get the worst part of the deal. Swallowing pride and smoothly losing of contention and conceding that you weren't right – regardless of whether you are unbiasedly right – just as saying sorry for getting distraught for obviously being wronged are both essential forfeits that you need to make to keep the harmony.

One of you may wind up doing this more often than not, while the other just infrequently does it, yet as long as it's simply the seemingly insignificant details and you are commonly upbeat, it doesn't generally make a difference.

22. One flatmate/accomplice will assume a lot of the work in certain regions, and that is OK

Talking about getting the worst part of the deal, with regards to things like keeping the house clean, planning dinners, outings to the store, pressing or fixing things around the home, one accomplice or flatmate will be increasingly competent or have a more noteworthy tender loving care than the other.

It will immediately become obvious who is slick and clean, who is the jack of all trades and who is somewhat of a lazy pig, however, can fix the PC, and so on. Let everybody do a lot of the work in a zone they are acceptable at and that they discover normal, rather than attempting to isolate all errands and undertakings directly down the center.

23. Try not to pester people, lecture or give them undesirable exercises

In the event that you need something done, simply tell people that. On the off chance that you are disappointed with something, enlighten them regarding it. Simply don't lecture or demand that things be done precisely the same way you do it since you are utilized to it, and there is no consistent or strategic explanation not to do it some other way. Be succinct while communicating your dismay and don't take up a fierce tone directly off the bat.

24. Never settle on ill-advised choices or start discussions when you are feeling irate or surly

Never hit the hay irate with your accomplice, never make a call or start a discussion when furious or ill-humored and never settle on any genuine choices until you have chilled off – live by these guidelines and you will do significantly less moronic things that you wind up lamenting.

25. Do some voyaging and experience different societies

You can go out traveling with companions, your darling, your family, or a blend of any of these. Having the option to have fun liberated from pressure and your standard commitments, all while encountering an entirely different culture, will help fortify and renew your relationship, and you may gain proficiency with certain things about one another you never knew.

None of this is such hard to get a handle on. However, a few focuses might be hard for people to acknowledge, and they will be extremely hard to execute. It takes a mess of dedication and persistence, however in the event that you remain centered and attempt to follow these guidelines each and every day, your life will slowly improve, and you will turn out to be a lot more joyful.

OVERCOME NEGATIVE EMOTIONS

Negative emotions can be portrayed as any inclination, which makes you be hopeless and dismal. These emotions make you hate yourself as well as other people, and remove your certainty.

Emotions that can become negative are detested, anger, envy, and trouble. However, in the correct setting, these emotions are totally common. Negative emotions can hose our eagerness forever, contingent upon to what extent we let them influence us and the manner in which we decide to communicate them.

Negative emotions prevent us from speculation and carrying on objectively and seeing circumstances in their actual viewpoint. When this happens, we will, in general, observe just what we need to see and recall just what we need to recollect. This just delays the anger or pain and keeps us from appreciating life.
The more drawn out this goes on, the more settled in the problem becomes. Managing negative emotions improperly can likewise be unsafe - for instance, communicating anger with viciousness.

It's essential to recognize what a feeling is and what an inclination is. While the two are interconnected, there's a greater distinction than you may understand. It's certainly something that shocked me when I started with my exploration.

Emotions – Emotions are viewed as 'lower level' reactions. They initially happen in the subcortical regions of the cerebrum, for example, the amygdala and the ventromedial prefrontal cortices. These territories are liable for delivering biochemical responses that directly affect your physical state.

Emotions are coded into our DNA and are thought to have created as an approach to assist us with reacting rapidly to various natural dangers, much like our 'battle or flight' reaction. The amygdala has additionally been appeared to assume a job in the arrival of synapses that are fundamental for memory, which is the reason emotional recollections are regularly more grounded and simpler to review.

Emotions have a more grounded physical establishing than sentiments meaning scientists discover them simpler to quantify dispassionately through physical signals, for example, blood flow, pulse, mind action, outward appearances, and non-verbal communication.

Sentiments – Emotions are viewed as going before sentiments, which will, in general, be our responses to the various emotions we experience. Where emotions can have a progressively summed up understanding over all people, sentiments are increasingly abstract and are affected by our own encounters and translations of our reality dependent on those encounters.

Sentiments happen in the neocortical districts of the mind and are the following stage by the way we react to our emotions as a person. Since they are so abstract, they can't be estimated the manner in which emotions can.

Negative emotions devour your internal vitality and harmony and take your present from your life. The most threatening problem of these emotions is that once you begin contemplating them, they begin to collect to an ever-increasing extent and become more grounded, which will make it harder to change. In the event that you know a couple of deceives, you can undoubtedly overwhelm your unfriendly emotions and accomplish anything you desire from your life.

Incredible tips for conquering your negative emotions:

1. Face the mirror

It is a typical wonder that people can see the truth about himself/herself just by remaining before the mirror. This case stands valid if there should be an occurrence of negative reasoning as well. At whatever point you feel yourself to be the captive of your emotions that harms you, remain before the mirror and set out to investigate your eyes in the mirror.

You will see your dull face because of that pessimism inside your mind. Furthermore, as you come to realize that you are getting dull, begin stimulating your perfect representation. Lift him to remove that reasoning. It has been seen that an individual can play out an errand just when he wants to carry out that responsibility. Like that, when you see yourself inside the mirror, your mind will quit bringing negative considerations, and in invert to that, it will begin boosting your spirit to stimulate.

"Negative emotions like scorn, demolish our significant serenity."

2. Review your cheerful minutes

Regardless of whether it is a cheerful event or a tragic one, recollections are made to charm you. There are numerous circumstances when your negative emotions begin harming your inward harmony. All things considered, old and upbeat recollections are the best cure. At whatever point you feel troubled, begin reviewing your most joyful minutes. In practically no time, you will see a grin all over. Another appeal will supplant the bluntness.

3. Get encompassed by bright people

Dejection is the home for negative emotions. The best option for it is to change your condition. At whatever point you feel like negative estimations, and you are distant from everyone else, go out to some down to earth region. You can consider your companions and run a social affair. All things considered, as far as science, at whatever point an undertaking is dispensed to the mind, it quits chipping away at the current one and starts contemplating the new assignment you put in your core interest. Your mind will get going on arranging the gathering with your companions, and all your dangerous emotions will reach a conclusion.

4. Start your leisure activity

At the point when you get yourself awkward due to negative emotions, begin doing your leisure activity. Numerous people love to understand books, many love to sing, others love to tune in to music. Every one of these side interests is the best medication to check unfavorable emotions present inside your body.

When you notice pessimism, start your pastime, as for instance, begin perusing a book you love to peruse. Your mind will naturally get occupied from reviewing negative considerations. Additionally, by perusing your preferred book, your mind just as your body will feel loose and positive emotions begin to start inside you.

5. Seek after meditation/yoga

It has been experimentally demonstrated that meditation is the best prescription for every single mind related problems. Regardless of whether you are experiencing low fixation or you are having a lot of unfriendly estimations inside yourself, meditation has the best result. Begin thinking by shutting your eyes. Inside murkiness, attempt to focus on a fanciful wellspring of light. Meditation is proposed to the people of each age gathering.

The primary utilization of pondering is to bring freshness into your mind. With ordinary practice, you will have the option to control your considerations, and as you will end up being the ace of your mind, there won't be any pessimism inside your mind. Along these lines, starting now and into the foreseeable future, include meditation or yoga inside your everyday schedule. The best time to perform them is promptly in the first part of the day.

6. Peruse positive statements

Your mind thinks cynical simply because of thrashing, however, with each annihilation, you got an encounter of how you can't win your fight. Imagine a scenario in which you direct your mind to just have positive emotions. It will act as needs be. In the event that you need inspiration, you need positive sentiments. To get positive sentiments, you need some positive sources to peruse. Perusing inspirational statements is a decent choice. The web is loaded up with crowded persuasive, uplifting citations. Begin guessing what those statements that implement you might be thinking of creating effective emotions every day.

"The indication of shrewd people is their capacity to control their emotions by the utilization of reason."

7. Begin chuckling

We, as a whole, realize that chuckling is the best drug. At whatever point, cynical emotions overwhelm your mind, leave everything aside, and begin giggling boisterously. It might sound senseless. However, this is otherwise called snickering treatment to take life back to miserable people. To change over your negative emotions into positive ones, go to a position of harmony and begin snickering boisterously. Giggle misleadingly once, twice, or multiple times. Later you will consequently begin chuckling normally. To actualize this, you should not make a big deal about what others will say subsequent to seeing me giggle this way.

With these previously mentioned brilliant tips, you can overwhelm your negative emotions and shape them into positive emotions.

8.   Origin.

Attempt to decide every circumstance that created negative reasoning. It is imperative to have the option to separate the minutes that trigger these kinds of musings. The problem isn't what you told or what occurs, however the relationship you have with your life. It might happen that it reminds you of some phase in your life. Or then again that you consider that you are thought little of. Or on the other hand that you don't confide in yourself. It is fundamental to attempt to recognize the beginning to have the option to conquer it.

The Health Benefits of effectively preparing emotions

The capacity to travel from the battle or flight modus (high in adrenalin) to the quiet and substance modus (high in oxytocin) is genuine expertise that we Westerners are not normally accepted at. We will, in general, often be in the 'stress state' or the 'endeavoring state' in which we make objectives, seek after them and experience brief highs from accomplishing them and the 'unsatisfied condition' of feeling on edge, disappointed and critical. This state is effortlessly activated when we neglect to accomplish our objectives.

The 'quiet and substance state' is one we battle to enter and seldom allow ourselves to be in. Our failure to turn on this quieting and relieving state puts substantial weight on our resistant framework just as our physical and emotional prosperity. We deny our bodies and mind the chance to quiet down and revive, leaving us inclined to pressure, wear out, despondency, and tension.

Emotional intelligence can lead us on the way to a satisfied and cheerful life by giving a structure through which to apply principles of intelligence to emotional reactions and comprehend that these reactions might be legitimately steady or conflicting with specific convictions about feeling.

As the workplace advances, so too does the group of research supporting that people (from assistants to chiefs) with higher EI are better prepared to work strongly inside groups, manage change all the more effectively, and oversee pressure – hence empowering them to all the more proficiently seek after business goals.

Emotions can assume a significant job by the way we think and carry on. The emotions we feel every day can force us to make a move and impact the choices we make about our lives, both huge and little. So as to genuinely get emotions, it is essential to comprehend the three basic parts of a feeling.

There are three sections to a feeling:

1. An abstract part (how you experience the feeling)

2. A physiological part (how your bodies respond to the feeling)

3. An expressive part (how you carry on because of the feeling).

These various components can assume a job in the capacity and motivation behind your emotional reactions.

Emotions can be brief, for example, a glimmer of inconvenience at a colleague, or durable, for example, suffering misery over the departure of a relationship. Be that as it may, why precisely do we experience emotions? What job do they serve?

Emotions Can Motivate Us to Take Action

At the point when confronted with a nerve-wracking test, you may feel a great deal of tension about whether you will perform well and how the test will affect your last grade. Due to these emotional reactions, you may be bound to contemplate. Since you encountered a specific feeling, you had the inspiration to make a move and plan something positive for improving your odds of getting a passing mark.

We likewise will, in general, take certain activities so as to encounter positive emotions and limit the likelihood of feeling negative emotions. For instance, you may search out social exercises or side interests that furnish you with a feeling of happiness, satisfaction, and fervor. Then again, you would presumably avoid circumstances that may conceivably prompt weariness, pity, or nervousness.

Emotions Help Us Survive, Thrive, and Avoid Danger

Naturalist Charles Darwin accepted that emotions are adjustments that allow the two people and creatures to endure and imitate. At the point when we are furious, we are probably going to defy the wellspring of our disturbance. At the point when we experience fear, we are bound to escape the danger. At the point when we feel loved, we may search out a mate and repeat.

Emotions serve a versatile job in our lives by persuading us to act rapidly and take activities that will augment our odds of endurance and achievement.

Emotions Can Help Us Make Decisions

Our emotions affect the choices we make, from what we choose to have for breakfast to which applicants we decide to decide in favor of in political decisions.

Scientists have additionally discovered that people with particular kinds of cerebrum harm influencing their capacity to encounter emotions likewise have a diminished capacity to use sound judgment.

Indeed, even in circumstances where we accept our choices are guided simply by rationale and discernment, emotions assume a key job. Emotional intelligence, or our capacity to comprehend and oversee emotions, has been appeared to assume a significant job in dynamic.

Emotions Allow Other People to Understand Us

At the point when we collaborate with others, it is critical to offer pieces of information to assist them with seeing how we are feeling. These prompts may include emotional demeanor through non-verbal communication, for example, different outward appearances associated with the specific emotions we are encountering.

In different cases, it may include legitimately expressing how we feel. At the point when we tell companions or relatives that we are feeling glad, tragic, energized, or alarmed, we are giving them significant data that they would then be able to use to make a move.

Emotions Allow Us to Understand Others

Similarly, as our own emotions give important data to other people, the emotional articulations of everyone around us give us an abundance of social data. Social correspondence is a significant piece of our day by day lives and connections, and having the option to decipher and respond to the emotions of others is basic. It allows us to react suitably and assemble further, increasingly significant associations with our companions, family, and friends and family. It likewise allows us to impart effectively in an assortment of social circumstances, from managing an angry client to dealing with a hot-headed worker.

Emotional showcases could likewise assume significant job insecurity and endurance. On the off chance that you experienced a murmuring or spitting creature, it would plainly show that the animal was furious and protective, prompting you to ease off and avoid conceivable danger.

Understanding the emotional showcases of others gives us clear data about how we may need to react in a specific circumstance....

DEVELOP SELF-CONTROL

Self-control is characterized as the capacity to deal with your activities, sentiments, and emotions. A case of self-control is the point at which you need the last treat however you utilize your resolve to avoid eating it since you realize it isn't beneficial for you

Self-control, a part of inhibitory control, is the capacity to direct one's emotions, contemplations, and conduct even with allurements and driving forces. As an official capacity, self-control is a psychological procedure that is important for directing one's conduct so as to accomplish explicit objectives.

A related idea in brain science is emotional self-guideline. Self-control is believed to resemble a muscle. As indicated by examines, self-guideline, regardless of whether emotional or social, was demonstrated to be a restricted asset which capacities like vitality. For the time being, abuse of self-control will prompt consumption. Notwithstanding, in the long haul, the utilization of self-control can reinforce and improve after some time.

Self-control is something we catch wind of constantly. Regularly, we consider it with regards to halting conduct we detest, such as eating lousy nourishment, or with regards to dealing with a having a feeling that anger. Nonetheless, the genuine definition goes past these thoughts. Here is simply the genuine significance control.

Self-control is "restriction practiced over one's driving forces, emotions, or wants." at the end of the day, we can keep ourselves from accomplishing something we would prefer not to do or from feeling something we would prefer not to feel, particularly when we're enticed.

It's an unimaginably supportive ability. For instance, when a specialist asks a patient to get more fit, self-control keeps them from eating a lot of lousy nourishment. On the off chance that they have to go to the exercise center, it likewise shields them from staring at the TV. At the point when somebody has a significant task or an undertaking due soon, they may delay except if they have enough self-control.

Emotional self-control is significant, as well. It keeps us from shouting at others when we're furious or from punching somebody when they wrong us. It likewise prevents us from crying uncontrollably when we don't get our path or from getting diverted in circumstances that require consideration.

In spite of the fact that we figure out how to self-mitigate as children (by, for instance, sucking on a pacifier), we're not brought into the world with self-control. We build up this ability all through our youth and apparently our whole lives. This is the reason it's not uncommon to see an irritated little child toss a toy over the room. However, similar conduct would be unusual in a grown-up.

Now and then, be that as it may, people arrive at adulthood with excessively little or an excessive amount of self-control. Neither one of the situations is perfect. Notwithstanding the physical and emotional difficulties this may bring, excessively little or a lot of self-control can likewise have social and mental impacts like disconnection, melancholy, or uneasiness. You may be considering what a healthy measure of self-control resembles, however, to best get that, it's imperative to recognize what to an extreme or too little resembles first.

Indications Of Too Much Self-Control

Self-control is generally a quality that people appreciate. Notwithstanding, when somebody has a lot of it, they can battle. Once in a while, people experiencing exorbitant self-control put on a show of being fussbudgets or appear to be tyrannical. Specialists call this conduct "over control." Someone managing "over control" might encounter the following:

- Difficulty unwinding

- Distance toward others

- Rigid character

- Overly centered on subtleties.

- Lack of sentiments or show of emotions

- Being capable (to say the least)

- Avoidance of hazard

By and large, people with a lot of self-control don't stand apart as much as the individuals who need self-control. Why? Since their conduct is regularly mistaken for being persevering, withdrawn, or highly reasonable. In view of that, how would we know whether somebody has an excessive amount of self-control or is basically fully grown? All things considered, it

In the event that somebody's conduct works for them and makes little no misery, all things considered, all is well. In any case, if inordinate self-control makes their physical, mental, emotional, or public activity a test, they may profit by observing an authorized guide.

Indications Of Too Little Self-Control

Somebody who needs self-control is anything but difficult to spot. They by and large experience issues focusing on positive propensities, and they will be unable to direct their sentiments or activities just as their companions. Indications of low self-control could be:

- Little or no self-discipline

- Lack of objectives or failure to arrive at objectives

- Low inspiration

- Little to no self-control

- Difficulty controlling emotions

- Lack of consideration

- Quick to accuse others

- Difficulty looking after kinships

- Dangerous or excessively uninvolved lifestyle

Having minimal self-control (or none by any stretch of the imagination) majorly affects one's everyday life. In addition to the fact that it is hard to manufacture self-certainty, but at the same time, it's difficult to work with others and arrive at objectives. On the off chance that somebody runs into similar obstructions, again and again, they may need to deal with self-control. Likewise, on the off chance that they appear to need a course or seem youthful, too minimal self-control may be the reason.

Step by step instructions to Have Self-Control

Everybody has an alternate measure of self-control, and it can change by circumstance, as well. However, the vast majority of us could utilize a lift to locate a superior harmony between excessively little and to an extreme. Here are a couple of tips to kick you off.

Unwind

It tends to be difficult to have self-control when we stunt ourselves into intuition. Something must be done desperately or halted right away. We likewise battle with self-control when we're driven by our gut responses. Envision you're driving not far off at high speed, and a slow driver cuts you off. Your gut response is the thing that makes you need to blare your horn and shout at them or more terrible.

To give yourself the most obvious opportunity at a more quiet reaction and a superior day, figure out how to slow your musings, so you can delay your gut motivations. Unwinding can help. Meditation, profound breathing, and mindfulness are altogether phenomenal approaches to rehearse unwinding. The more you unwind, the almost certain you are to tranquility move toward distressing occasions and pick attentive reactions as opposed to following up on drive alone.

Figure out how To Plan

Self-control is difficult to accomplish without heading. For instance, on the off chance that you need to shed 10 pounds, and in this way you need to skirt your daily pastry, it assists with preparing. Rather than trusting you'll be sufficient when the opportunity arrives, consider approaches to control your hunger ahead of time, so you're bound to succeed.

To avoid depending on self-control, make an arrangement for what you will do whenever you're tired. Maybe you can anticipate completing 15 minutes of yoga or perusing a decent book when you have a hankering for sugar. Utilizing interruptions like this can assist you with improving your self-control over the long haul. You will, in the end, discover that you can beat disagreeable emotions and that you don't have to follow up on the entirety of your wants.

Discover What You Want

At times we need self-control since we're not clear on precisely what we need. For instance, in the event that it feels like you're going no place in your present place of employment, ensure it's not on the grounds that you don't have the foggiest idea where you need to go straight away. At the point when you have an unmistakable objective, it's simpler to practice self-control since you can settle on decisions that point you the correct way.

So, it's essential to have objectives that are significant to you. Try not to set an objective since some other person or thing pushes you toward it. Peer profound inside yourself, and discover why your objective issues to you. In the event that it doesn't mean anything to you, it will be extremely difficult to commit yourself to it.

Recall The Consequences

Look past transient delight, and consider the long haul esteem. On the off chance that you set yourself up for progress by dealing with yourself tomorrow, your self-control will normally develop after some time as you begin to receive the rewards.

Pretend

On the off chance that rehearsing self-control is a test for you, pretend with a companion, a relative, or a specialist. This will assist you with standing up to your emotions in a controlled domain without the risk of negative results. To begin, consider a straightforward circumstance where you normally battle with self-control. As your self-control improves, branch out to progressively troublesome or testing circumstances.

Get Healthy

Similarly, as with any proactive conduct, being in the privilege, physical, mental, and the emotional spot has a major effect. In the event that it's been some time since your last physical test, call you are essential health care doctor and timetable an arrangement. A hidden condition may be intensifying your self-control issues. With that in mind, in case you're encountering indications of sorrow, tension, or other emotional well-being issues, kindly get help right away.

What's more, by and large, make sure to deal with the rudiments. Eat a healthy eating routine, drink a lot of water, and get approximately eight hours of rest for every night. This will assist you with keeping a reasonable mind on your excursion to better self-control.

Self-control assumes a significant job in our lives, and it's frequently a major factor in our general degrees of fulfillment. While it's conceivable to show a lot of self-control, an absence of self-control will, in general, push us into difficulty.

HOW TO HAVE SELF CONTROL

1. Self-Monitor

On the off chance that you can screen yourself, you will have the option to monitor your own conduct and see where you might be coming up short and where you are succeeding.

Monitoring this will assist you with making changes to specific propensities that might be upsetting you and making you lose your self-control.

It additionally shows you, then again, what you are doing that is sure.

Self-checking is an extraordinary method to keep criticism all alone conduct, which will make it simpler to assess and monitor how well you are getting along in specific circumstances and what you can change.

2. A Can-Do Attitude

Having a superior, progressively inspirational mentality towards our objectives and life can assist us with focusing and manage pressure much better.

For instance, it can assist us with developing tolerance and self-control when something turns out badly.

This is an incredible self-control strategy, which can assist you with having an alternate way to deal with things, for example, feeling like you can accomplish your objectives and that they are not out of your range.

Having a can-do disposition can keep you in good shape to having the option to remain in control, to be tolerant, and to concentrate on accomplishing what you need to accomplish.

3. Pre-Commit

Having the option to subscribe to your objectives will help a ton when you really endeavor to contact them. On the off chance that you can focus on a choice before making it, it ought to be a lot simpler to make.

For instance, on the off chance that you focus on eating healthier, you will think that its a lot simpler on the off chance that you make the dedication already to do your week after week looking for healthier nourishments and settling on a choice to not eat out.

In the event that you have not submitted and, for example, have chosen to keep a cabinet of unhealthy nourishments, you are more averse to have self-control and may have set yourself up for disappointment. Pre-submitting is an extraordinary method to keep concentrated on your objectives and make it simpler for yourself to accomplish them.

4. Use Rewards

Utilizing prizes can truly help with your self-control. In the event that we realize that there is something toward the finish of your objective to remunerate you, we are ordinarily bound to do it.

Having a momentary penance will appear to be substantially more sensible when we realize that there is a prize (an increase) for us toward its finish.

This is an incredible self-control system, as it will assist with keeping you roused and will give you a motivating force to accomplish your objectives and to remain concentrated on them. This will likewise assist you with being quiet, as you will realize that in the event that you carry on, there will be a compensation toward the end, and you will be less inclined to lose your self-control.

5. Self-Affirmations

Self-certifications are certain sentences that you can rehash to yourself, this is an extraordinary self-control procedure, one that is likewise spoken about when utilizing the Law Of Attraction.

At the point when you rehash positive insistences, for example, things you are appreciative of, things you have accomplished or need to accomplish, your center convictions, and so on, it keeps you in an increasingly uplifting mindset. This, thus, will keep you spurred as you can consider what you have just accomplished or things that you are grateful for.

At the point when you are concentrating on your positive convictions, it can help with remaining on track and being understanding when attempting to arrive at your objectives. After you have rehashed your insistences to yourself, you should feel like you have the correct demeanor to arrive at your objectives and remain positive.

This can likewise give you the inspiration to continue, as you will have the option to add your new objectives to your assertions once you have accomplished them.

Simple Ways To Increase Your Self-Control

You can increase more noteworthy self-control in all circumstances by utilizing these master tips and exhortation upheld by logical research.

Here's a ton we can do to alleviate resolve exhaustion and improve our capacity to practice self-control, including the following eight hints.

1. Take a gander at the comprehensive view.

High-level reasoning advances self-control achievement. That is, people are bound to practice self-control when they see the famous timberland past the trees and when they don't get hindered by explicit particulars.

For instance, when dealing with a long haul venture, it's anything but difficult to get disappointed by the huge number of little advances required to get you there. Rather, occasionally reminding yourself as well as other people in the group of the ultimate objective serves to advance self-control by forestalling debilitation.

2. Know the dangers of lacking rest.

The lack of sleep channels glucose in the prefrontal cortex, in this way, draining the fuel required for self-control. Rest reestablishes it. This was found to have any kind of effect at work the following day among moral and dishonest conduct, for example, cheating by distorting receipts. The individuals who dozed six hours or less were bound to take part in degenerate work practices than the individuals who rested over six hours.

The suggestions for those maintaining a business are too imperative to even think about ignoring. "Associations," says the lead scientist Christopher M. Barnes, "need to give rest more regard. Administrators and supervisors should remember that the more they push representatives to work late, go to the workplace early, and answer messages and calls at painfully inconvenient times, the more they welcome untrustworthy conduct to sneak in." Are you driving your people excessively hard? Do you urge colleagues to organize rest in their lives? Do you set a genuine model yourself? Tired laborers are bad for business.

3. Loosen up as of now.
Famous perspectives on self-control are that we should attempt to control driving forces, battle enticements, and effectively practice resolve. Nothing could be further from reality, it appears. People prepared with words proposing activity, for example, "start," or "continue ahead with it," were more probable than others to settle on incautious choices that undermine their long haul objectives. Interestingly, those prepared to "rest" or "stop" thought that it was simpler to avoid imprudent choices. The casual state is better at restraining the draw of allurements." This might just have some effect on the way we oversee people. Pushing them to "proceed

onward" may bring about increasingly hazardous conduct or rash choices.

4. Do some short episodes of activity.

Do you wind up with restricted time to embrace a full exercise program? Fortunately, with regards to self-control, short episodes of reasonably exceptional exercise are all you have to support your quality right now. The pre-frontal cortex is liable for self-control. Expanded blood and oxygen flow to the pre-frontal cortex, which may clarify the lift in self-control capacity. Regardless of how bustling you are, plan to remember a short explosion of activity for your everyday schedule.

5. Gain computerized self-power support.

There is plenty of applications that can assist you with practicing self-control, even applications that can assist you with showing control when you're on the web. There are numerous different approaches to assist you with re-appropriating your self-control: a self-coercing administration to help shield you from stopping—regardless of whether it's composing a blog or shedding pounds; Stick.com that keeps you focused on any objective; GymPact to guarantee you never miss another exercise, just as other comparable applications to follow your exercises; and Mint.com or Expense Manager to monitor you are going through and assist you with bringing in better cash choices.

6. Know yourself.

Emotional self-control, or motivation control, are foundations of emotional intelligence. Know yourself so you can deal with your emotions and driving forces. For instance, would you say you are prone to respond hurriedly to issues? When you begin, do you think that its difficult to quit talking? Is it true that you are ready to remain created and positive in upsetting conditions? Would you be able to practice tolerance in irritating circumstances? The capacity to hold problematic emotions and motivations under tight restraints is the characteristic of a prepared pioneer.

Self-mindfulness goes before self-administration. Here are two emotional intelligence appraisals to assist you with expanding your self-information right now: Emotional Quotient Inventory and the Emotional Competence Inventory.

7. Avoid choice weakness.

Self-control has significant ramifications in the nature of our choices. After people have settled on various choices, regardless of how little they've spent their resolve, and their self-control is undermined. Choice weakness negatively affects our choices. For instance, a few people respond by inclining toward not to settle on a choice by any means; others may settle on indiscreet choices or choices that are increasingly dependent upon nonsensical predisposition. Avoid settling on choices about significant issues by the day's end, when you have just settled on a huge number of choices as we as a whole do during the typical course of a day. For instance, it shows that a few judges in court have been known to settle on more unfortunate choices by the day's end.

Put some part of your life on default mode, so you don't need to settle on such a large number of superfluous choices. Steve Jobs, for instance, constantly wearing 501 pants and dark turtlenecks. President Obama wears just blue or dark suits. "I'm attempting to pare down choices. "I would prefer not to settle on choices about what I'm eating or wearing. Since I have such a large number of different choices to make ... You have to center your dynamic vitality. You have to routinize yourself. You can't be experiencing the day occupied by incidental data." Take motivation from this to perceive what you can do to streamline dynamic in the more everyday parts of your life.

8. Taste some lemonade.

The job of glucose in self-control. Glucose is the concoction in the circulatory system that conveys vitality to the mind, muscles, and different organs and frameworks. "In straightforward terms," Baumeister says, "glucose is fuel for the mind. Demonstrations of self-control lessen blood glucose levels. Low degrees of glucose foresee horrible showing on self-control undertakings and tests." Willpower can be reestablished by raising your glucose. Intermittently renewing glucose, regardless of whether it's simply with a glass of lemonade, to fortify your capacity to keep up self-control.

How to Develop and Practice Self-Regulation

How Stress Impacts Your Health

Self-guideline can be characterized in different manners. In the most fundamental sense, it includes controlling one's conduct, emotions, and contemplations in the quest for long haul objectives. All the more explicitly, emotional self-guideline alludes to the capacity to oversee troublesome emotions and motivations. At the end of the day, to think before acting. It additionally mirrors the capacity to perk yourself up after frustrations and to act in a manner steady with your most profound held qualities.

Advancement of Self-Regulation

Your capacity to self-manage as a grown-up has established in your advancement during adolescence. Figuring out how to self-manage is significant expertise that kids learn both for emotional development and later social associations.

In a perfect circumstance, a baby who pitches fits develops into a kid who figures out how to endure awkward emotions without having a tantrum and later into a grown-up who can control motivations to act dependent on awkward sentiments. Generally, development mirrors the capacity to confront emotional, social, and intellectual dangers in the earth with tolerance and attentiveness. In the event that this portrayal reminds you of mindfulness, that is no mishap—mindfulness does surely identify with the capacity to self-control.

Importance

Self-guideline includes taking an interruption between an inclination and a move—setting aside the effort to thoroughly consider things, make an arrangement, stand by quietly. Kids frequently battle with these practices, and grown-ups should.

It's anything but difficult to perceive how an absence of self-guideline will mess up life. A kid who shouts or hits other youngsters out of disappointment won't be mainstream among peers and may confront censures at school. A grown-up with poor self-guideline aptitudes may need self-certainty and self-esteem and experience difficulty taking care of pressure and dissatisfaction. Frequently, this may be communicated regarding anger or tension, and increasingly serious cases might be analyzed as a psychological issue.

Self-guideline is additionally significant in that it allows you to act as per your profoundly held qualities or inner social voice and to communicate properly. In the event that you esteem scholastic accomplishment, it will allow you to consider rather than slack off before a test. On the off chance that you esteem helping other people, it will allow you to help an associate with a task, regardless of whether you are on a tight cutoff time yourself.

In its most essential structure, self-guideline allows us to skip once more from disappointment and remain quiet under tension. These two capacities will help you through life, more than different abilities.

Normal Problems

How do problems with self-guideline create? It could begin right on time; as a baby being ignored. A youngster who doesn't have a sense of security and secure, or who is uncertain whether their needs will be met, may experience difficulty mitigating and self-regulating.1

Afterward, a youngster, adolescent, or grown-up may battle with self-guideline, either in light of the fact that this capacity was not created during adolescence or due to an absence of methodologies for overseeing troublesome sentiments. At the point when left unchecked, after some time, this could prompt increasingly major issues, for example, psychological well-being issues and unsafe practices, for example, substance misuse.

Effective Strategies

In the event that self-guideline is so significant, for what reason were the vast majority of us never shown methodologies for utilizing this expertise? Regularly, guardians, instructors, and different grown-ups expect that youngsters will "develop out of" the fit of the rage stage. While this is valid generally, all kids and grown-ups can profit by learning solid procedures for self-guideline.

Mindfulness

Mindfulness is "the mindfulness that emerges from focusing, deliberately, right now and non-judgementally." By participating in aptitudes, for example, centered breathing and appreciation, mindfulness empowers us to put some space among ourselves and our responses, prompting better concentration and sentiments of tranquility and unwinding.

Mindfulness was appeared to improve consideration, which thus assisted with controlling negative emotions and official working (higher-request thinking).

Intellectual Reappraisal

Intellectual reappraisal or subjective reframing is another system that can be utilized to develop self-guideline capacities. This procedure includes changing your idea designs. In particular, subjective reappraisal includes reconsidering a circumstance so as to change your emotional reaction to it. For instance, envision a companion who didn't restore your calls or messages for a few days. As opposed to feeling this reflected something important to you, for example, "my companion loathes me," you may rather figure, "my companion must be truly occupied."

Utilizing subjective reappraisal in regular day to day existence is identified with encountering and progressively positive and more positive emotions. The connection between self-guideline systems (i.e., mindfulness, subjective reappraisal, and feeling concealment) and emotional prosperity, scientists saw psychological reappraisal as related to every day positive emotions, including sentiments of eagerness, happiness, fulfillment, and energy.

Some other valuable techniques for self-guideline incorporate acknowledgment and problem-illuminating. Conversely, unhelpful techniques that people some of the time use incorporate avoidance, interruption, concealment, and stress.

Characteristics of Self-Regulators

The advantages of self-guideline are various. As a rule, people who are adroit at self-managing will, in general, observe the positive qualities in others, see difficulties as circumstances, keep up open correspondence, are clear about their goals, demonstration as per their qualities, set forth their best exertion, prop up through troublesome occasions, stay adaptable and adjust to circumstances, assume responsibility for circumstances when essential, and can quiet themselves when vexed and cheer themselves when feeling down.

The most effective method to Put Self-Regulation Into Practice

You are most likely reasoning that it sounds brilliant to be acceptable at self-controlling. However, you, despite everything, don't have a clue about how to improve your abilities.

In kids, guardians can help create self-guideline through schedules (e.g., set certain eating times, have a lot of practices for every movement). Schedules help kids realize what's in store, which causes it simpler for them to feel good. At the point when youngsters act in manners that don't exhibit self-guideline, disregard their solicitations, for example, by making them pause in the event that they interfere with a discussion.

As a grown-up, the initial step to rehearse self-guideline is to perceive that everybody has a decision in how to respond to circumstances. While you may feel like life has given you a terrible hand, it's not the hand you are managed, yet how you respond to it that issues most. How precisely do you gain proficiency with this aptitude of self-guideline?

Perceive that in each circumstance, you have three alternatives: approach, avoidance, and assault. While it might feel as if your decision of conduct is out of your control, it's definitely not. Your sentiments may influence you more toward one way, yet you are more than those emotions.

The subsequent advance is to get mindful of your transient emotions. Do you want to flee from a troublesome circumstance? Do you want to lash out in anger at somebody who has harmed you? Screen your body to get pieces of information about how you are feeling on the off chance that it isn't quickly clear to you. For instance, a quickly expanding heart might be an indication that you are entering a condition of anger or a fit of anxiety.

Begin to re-establish harmony by concentrating on your profoundly held qualities, instead of those transient emotions. See past that distress right now to the bigger picture. At that point, a demonstration in a way that lines up with self-guideline.

When you've taken in this sensitive exercise in careful control, you will start to self-manage all the more regularly, and it will end up being a lifestyle for you. Creating self-guideline aptitudes will improve your strength and capacity to confront troublesome conditions in life. Nonetheless, on the off chance that you discover you can't instruct yourself to self-direct, think about visiting psychological well-being proficient. The time might be valuable to execute explicit techniques for your circumstance.

Tips for Managing Conflict, Tension, and Anger

Keeping up Your Composure When Your Buttons Are Being Pushed

Here are our best tips for overseeing struggle, strain, and anger. All things considered, to be a protected and unsurprising individual for people around you at work and at home, it is fundamental that you can keep up your poise when you sense that your catches are being pushed. This quality will assist you in achieving your objectives in business just as your objectives for your own connections.

Offer Negative Emotions Only in Person or on the Phone

Messages, replying mail messages, and notes are unreasonably generic for the sensitive idea of negative words.

Pepper Your Responses with the Phrase, "I Understand"

This expression will bolster your objectives when the strain is high, and you have to discover shared opinion to frame bargains or concurrences with the other party.

Pay heed When You Feel Threatened by What Someone Is Saying to You.

Oppose the impulse to protect yourself or to "shut down" the other individual's correspondence. It will take this sort of order to turn into an open, confiding in the communicator.

Work on Making Requests of Others When You Are Angry

It is regularly significantly more helpful to make a solicitation than to share your anger. For instance, if the sitter is making you insane by leaving messy dishes in the sink, it is smarter to make a solicitation of them than to let your anger spill out in different manners, for example, by getting progressively far off.

Have a go at Repeating the Exact Words That Someone Is Saying to You When They Are in a Lot of Emotional Pain or When You Disagree with Them Completely

This reflecting system can keep both the speaker and the audience 'focused' in a troublesome discussion, particularly when the demeanor of the individual doing the reflecting is to increase the comprehension of an alternate perspective.

Assume Liability for Your Feelings to Avoid Blaming Others

Notice while 'blameshifting' starts to spill into your discourse. "I feel irate when you are twenty minutes late, and you don't call me" is far superior to, "You make me so distraught by being late." Figure out how to Listen to the Two Sides of the Conflict That You Are in as though You Were the Mediator or the Counselor

On the off chance that you can tune in and react right now will carry harmony and answers for the contention all the more rapidly. For instance, in light of a worker's raise demand, you may state, "From one perspective I comprehend that you truly need the raise, and then again I speak to the organization, whose assets are rare right now. Is there a way that I can deal with your remuneration bundle that doesn't include money?" Here, the middle person's perspective can search for the innovative trade-off that considers the points of confinement and the requirements of the two gatherings.

Take a Playful Attitude Towards Developing the Skill of Emotional Self-Control in High Conflict Situations

You could see keeping up self-control in a strained, irate discussion as an athletic accomplishment. You could likewise see building up this ability as working out at the rec center with loads - the more that you utilize your self-control muscle, the greater it will develop, and the simpler it will be to resist the urge to panic when strain is incredible.

Hold up a Few Days to Cool Down Emotionally When a Situation Makes You Feel Wild with Intense Feelings, Such as Rage

Over the long haul, you will have the option to be progressively objective about the issues and to sift through reality with regards to the circumstance all the more unmistakably.

Settle on a Decision to Speak with Decorum Whenever You Are Angry or Frustrated

In the event that you give yourself consent to blow up, people won't have a sense of security around you. They will feel that you are not unsurprising and will convey 'shields' when they are close to you. The fear and dividers of others won't bolster your objectives for accomplishment seeing someone or at work.

CPSIA information can be obtained
at www.ICGtesting.com
Printed in the USA
BVHW090411210421
605393BV00004B/864

9 781802 342031